GCSE Media STUDIES for AQA

- Mandy Esseen
- Martin Phillips
- Anne Riley
- Consultant: Lesley Wisson

www.heinemann.co.uk

✓ Free online support
✓ Useful weblinks
✓ 24 hour online ordering

01865 888058

Heinemann

Inspiring generations

Integrated with
MediaStage by:

explore›discover›learn

Heinemann Educational Publishers
Halley Court, Jordan Hill, Oxford OX2 8EJ
Part of Harcourt Education

Heinemann is the registered trademark of
Harcourt Education Limited

© Harcourt Education Ltd, 2004

The authors and publishers would like to express their grateful
thanks to Lydia Hocking, an experienced teacher of Media Studies,
who wrote the excellent unit on pop music. The authors and
publishers would also like to thank the media students of Stanwell
School, Vale of Glamorgan, especially Sarah Millman, for their
contributions to this book. Finally, the authors and publishers are
indebted to Caroline Hannan – thank you, you are a star!

First published 2004

09 08 07 06 05
10 9 8 7 6 5 4 3 2

British Library Cataloguing in Publication Data is available
from the British Library on request.

ISBN 0 435 10969 3

Designed by Hicksdesign
Typeset by Kamae Design

Original illustrations © Harcourt Education Limited, 2004
Printed and bound in Italy by Printer Trento S.r.l
Cover photo: © Getty Images/Taxi

Every attempt has been made to ensure that all coursework
assignments meet the requirements of the AQA GCSE Media
Studies specification. However, teachers and students should refer to
the current specification for the most up-to-date requirements and
information.
(www.aqa.org.uk)

Acknowledgements
Every effort has been made to contact copyright holders of material
reproduced in this book. Any omissions will be rectified in
subsequent printings if notice is given to the publishers.

BBFC symbols (British Board of Film Classification). Reprinted with
the kind permission of BBFC; Extract from a review of *My Family*
from *Radio Times Guide to TV Comedy* by Mark Lewisohn (BBC
Worldwide 2003). Reprinted with the kind permission of the author;
Photo from *My Family*. Reprinted by permission of the BBC Photo
Archive; Extract from 'Fury as Mugabe shuts down the paper that
defied him' by Andrew Meldrum, *The Observer*, 14th September
2003. Copyright © Andrew Meldrum 2003. Reprinted with
permission of *The Observer*; Front page of *AsianXpress*; Front page
of *The Daily Express*, 21st November 2003; Front page of *The
Times*, 12th September 2001; Front page of *The Mirror*,
9th November 2000; Front cover of *NZZ*, 5th February 1999; Front
cover of *Le Télégramme*, No 17.077 11th April 2003; Front page of
The Daily Express, 6th October 1999; Front page of *The Mirror*,
6th October 1999; Front page of *The Daily Mail*, 6th October
1999; Estimates of average issue readership based on data collected
by the National Readership Survey. Reprinted with permission of
NRS Ltd; Front cover of *Now* magazine, 9th June 2004. Copyright
© NOW/IPC Syndication. Reprinted with the kind permission of IPC
Syndication; Front cover of *Hotdog* magazine, November 2003.

Reprinted with the kind permission of Paragon; Front cover of
Asiana Wedding, Summer 2004. Reprinted with the kind permission
of *Asiana* magazine; Front cover of *Mizz* magazine, November
2003. Copyright © MIZZ/IPC Syndication. Reprinted with the kind
permission of IPC Syndication; Contents page from *Dare* magazine,
11th–25th February 2004. Reprinted by permission of DARE
editorial/BBC; Extract from *The Outlaw*. Copyright © 1996 by
Joanne Ross. Excerpt reprinted with permission of Harlequin
Enterprises II B.V., Harlequin K.K. and Kabushiki Kaisha Ohzora
Shuppan; Extract from 'Big Yellow Taxi', words and music by Jack
Hammer & Otis Blackwell. Copyright © 1957 B.R.S. Music
Corporation. All rights assigned to Chappell & Company
Incorporated, USA. Carlin Music Corporation. All rights reserved.
International Copyright Secured; Front cover of *NME* magazine,
22nd May 2004. Copyright © NME/IPC Syndication. Reprinted with
the kind permission of IPC Syndication; Front cover of *Top of the
Pops Magazine*, issue 107, January 2004, and article 'A letter for
everyone'. Reprinted with the kind permission of Top of the Pops
Magazine/BBC; Article 'Alex Parks Style' from *CosmoGirl!* magazine
March 2004, pg 15. Courtesy of *CosmoGirl!* Copyright © National
Magazine Company. Reprinted with permission; Front cover from
Heat magazine, issue 251, 3rd–9th January 2004. Reprinted with
permission of EMAP; Two short quotes by James Oldham; Extract
from *Broadcasting Journalism: Techniques of Radio and TV News*
by Andrew Boyd, Focal Press, 1997. Reprinted with permission of
Elsevier Limited; Extracts and photographs relating to Gemini FM.
Reprinted with the kind permission of Gemini FM; Extracts from
RAJAR figures. Reprinted with the kind permission of RAJAR Ltd.;
Bazar perfume advert. Reprinted with the kind permission of
Kenneth Green Associates; Picture from Club 18-30 Summer 2005
Preview cover. Reprinted with the kind permission of Up Trips
Marketing; Nivea for men – sensitive skin advert. Reprinted with the
kind permission of Beiersdorf UK; WDCS advert. Reprinted with the
kind permission of WDCS and the photographer Mark Carwardine;
Image from *A Close Shave*. Copyright © Aardman/Wallace &
Gromit Ltd, 1995. Reprinted with permission of Aardman
Animations; Bertolli advertisements reproduced with the kind
permission of Unilever; 'Butler betrays Diana's Memory' from *The
Daily Express*, Tuesday 5th November 2002. Copyright © Express
Newspapers Limited. Reprinted with permission; 'Butler speaks out
only in The Mirror', *The Mirror*, Tuesday 5th November 2002.
Copyright © Mirror Newspapers. Reprinted with permission;
Newport News advert. Reprinted for educational purposes only with
permission of Newport News; Gasoline Blue Jeans advert.

**The publishers would like to thank the following for
permission to reproduce photographs on the pages noted.**

Alamy (pp19, 55**B**, 167); BBC (pp37, 39**T**); bbc.co.uk (p52); Corbis
(pp19, 31, 32, 116, 129**T**); Corbis/Bettmann (pp42, 51);
Corbis/Brendan Beime (p94**L**); Corbis/Chuck Savage (p122);
Corbis/Douglas Kirkland (p59); Corbis/Frank Trapper (p127**L**);
Corbis/Maiman Rick (p16); Corbis/Neal Preson (p119); Freemantle
Media Stills Library (pp46, 47**R**); Getty Images/Lonely Planet (p70**R**);
Getty Images/Photodisc (p70**L**); Harcourt Index (p153); Historical
Newspaper Loan Service/John Frost (pp63, 66, 69, 72, 76); Kobal
(pp14, 105); Kobal/20thcentury Fox & Paramount (pp27 figs 13, **14,
15**); Kobal/Dreamworks LLC (p112); Kobal/Universal (p15); Network
Seven, Australia (p47**L**); PA Photos (p125); PA Photos/Abaca (p92);
PA Photos/Abaca Press (p94**R**); PA Photos/David Cheskin (p45); PA
Photos/EPA (p134**R**); PA Photos/Neil Munns (p54); PA Photos/Sean
Dempsey (p134**L**); Redferns (pp127**R**, 129**B**, 132); Rex Features
(pp39**B**, 93); The Advertising Archive Ltd (pp100, 159); The
Freemantle Media Stills Library (p40); The Illustrated London News
Photo Library (p62); The Kobal Collection (pp103, 138); The Kobal
Collection/Touchstone (p27 **fig 12**); The Kobal Collection/20th
Century Fox TV (p53); The Kobal Collection/Amblin/Universal (p16);
The Kobal Collection/Columbia (p113); The Kobal
Collection/Columbia/Marvel (p30); The Kobal Collection/Dreamworks
LLC (p102); The Kobal Collection/Lawrence Gordon, Mutual Film,
Paramount/Alex Bailey (p101); The Kobal Collection/Lorimar (p158);
The Kobal Collection/Paramount (p43**L**); The Kobal
Collection/Paramount TV (p43**R**); The Kobal Collection/Universal
(p22); The Kobal Collection/Warner Bros TV (p48); The Ronald Grant
Archive (pp25, 28); Topfoto (p55**T**); www.britishbakeries.co.uk
(p160); www.fox.co.uk/buffy (p41). Other photographs are
reproduced by kind permission of Mandy Esseen and Martin Phillips.

Contents

The following icon is used in this book:

This indicates that an activity is available in *MediaStage*.

Introduction

Congratulations! You have joined the growing number of students who have chosen to study GCSE Media Studies and to find out about the fascinating world of the media and its important role in today's society.

What kinds of things do we study?

Your Media Studies course will encourage you to explore a range of media texts: products such as television programmes, magazines, radio shows and films. By learning about how they convey meaning, how they are made and who made them, you can become confident and skilled in making judgements and reflecting on what you have learned.

Do we get to make our own media texts?

Your course will also help you learn by giving you the chance to make media texts of your own; you can find out at first hand what skills are required to create productions that inform and entertain the audiences who will consume them.

Will we have the chance to show what we know?

The good news is that you begin the course with the advantage of having a great deal of knowledge about the media from your experience of the world around you and from your own choice of entertainment – the media products which are all around in everyday life. You will have the opportunity to channel this existing expertise and to use it to produce responses that show what you know, understand and can do.

What variety of texts will we learn about?

This book is designed to provide you with a wealth of examples of media texts to discuss and analyse. In addition, you will find up-to-date information about the trends in the media today. The study of texts from earlier times show developments in technology and changes in the social roles of individuals and groups in society, encouraging you to reflect upon the influences that have shaped our media today.

What about the work we give in?

Advice is given on how to approach both the written and practical work you will be required to submit as evidence of your achievement in Media Studies and which will be assessed for the GCSE qualification for which you are aiming.

Will the activities all be the same?

Everybody has a particular style of learning. Students who are sometimes called 'active learners' tend to retain and understand information best by doing something active with it – discussing or applying it or explaining it to others. Other students prefer a 'reflective' style that allows them to think about a topic quietly. A 'visual learner' responds to information presented in pictures and diagrams.

Everyone can be an active learner, a reflective learner and a visual learner, adopting particular styles at different times. It is therefore important to have a selection of approaches that stimulate and motivate and allow you to be confident about your learning. This book provides activities and tasks that are designed to match different styles and therefore allow you to learn most effectively. These include regular opportunities for discussion, working with visual materials and practical tasks as well as the more formal writing about ideas and facts.

How will we find out what we need to know to do well in our GCSE?

Examination boards produce specifications that are outlines of what is to be covered in the course and how it is to be assessed. The topic areas and activities in this book help you achieve these 'assessment objectives' by matching these requirements. Some of the activities help you explore ideas; others are assignments to be completed for formal assessment. Units 10–15 provide you with suggestions and support for these assignments. Together, they provide you with what you need to do well in your GCSE.

Will we need to know any special vocabulary?

Media Studies, like any other subject, has its own technical terms which are a kind of shorthand for explaining processes or ideas used in the media industry by the people who make products or those who study them. In order to help you with these specialist terms, there are boxes which explain key terms. Sometimes the terms cover key concepts – central ideas that are important in the study of a variety of topic areas.

In addition you will find Tip boxes that will help you to understand what examiners are looking for. Other Tip boxes will give you practical hints, or show you where and how you can do further research on the Internet.

Can we dip into the book at different points?

The design of the book allows you to approach each topic on its own or to follow the order of the units as you prefer. The units start with activities designed to get you thinking, then go into more detail. There are tasks, activities and questions at regular intervals. You will find that some material is covered several times in the book in different contexts – this is because these are important topics that you will need to understand in the first unit you tackle. The final part of the book provides you with lots of ideas for your assignments.

Can we use the Internet for research?

The Internet is a very useful resource for Media Studies. There are links to relevant websites in this book. In order to ensure that the links are up-to-date, that the links work, and that the sites are not inadvertently linked to sites that could be considered offensive, we have made the links available on the Heinemann website at www.heinemann.co.uk/hotlinks. When you access the site, the express code is **9693P**.

What is MediaStage?

MediaStage is a 3D animated learning environment designed for GCSE Media Studies. It is an exciting way for you to explore the key areas of media studies along with developing practical skills in film and television, and demonstrating understanding of theory.

MediaStage is, in essence, a virtual movie production kit where you can choose from a range of pre-made production sets, or even create your own using the range of layouts and props available.

You can choose from a cast of actors who can be placed within the set and animated using a range of gesture and movement instructions. You can use text-to-speech technology to make the characters say their lines, import pre-recorded audio, or use the recording facility to record your own voices for the part.

Once the performance is ready you can set up cameras and lighting. There is a range of editing tools that will allow you to record, play back and then modify your performances. You can bring your own 'real' video footage into your performances, and can also export your finished performances to video tape for more traditional editing.

Why use MediaStage *for GCSE Media Studies?*

By using *MediaStage* you will not only be developing practical media skills, you will also be putting into practice the theories and concepts you have learnt during your course. For example, you might create a narrative sequence to demonstrate your understanding of the five stages of Todorov's narrative theory.

It is not intended that *MediaStage* replaces other technology when you do production work – you will benefit from using 'real' digital video equipment or setting up 'real' photo shoots with live props and models. However, there are a huge variety of ways in which MediaStage can be used in a GCSE Media course, and it can complement other media technologies.

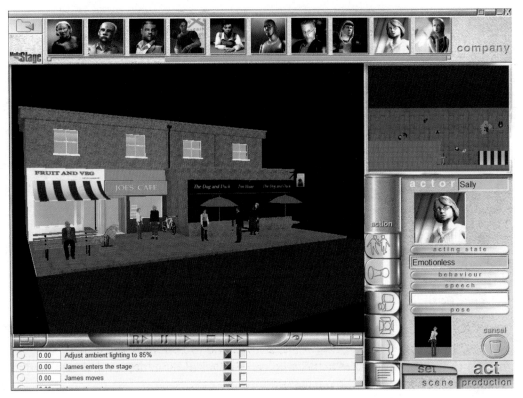

For example, one area where *MediaStage* can really enhance your work is by allowing you to create your 'ideal' sets for a film project. Very often students are limited to filming in, say, the school grounds and are frustrated because they cannot create professional-looking sets. Within *MediaStage* this problem is overcome, and sets can also be professionally lit. Even if you go on to film in a 'real' location, you can storyboard using still shots from *MediaStage* – this will greatly enhance the planning sections of any productions you undertake.

 This icon indicates that activities are available in *MediaStage*.

Introduction to GCSE Media Studies for AQA

First of all – welcome to the wonderful world of Media Studies. As the old knight says to Indiana Jones in *The Last Crusade*, 'You have chosen well'. During your GCSE course you will have many opportunities to study areas of the media which you will already know a great deal about. In fact, there can't be many subjects you will begin to study with so much previous knowledge. Part of the fun of this course is that you will learn how to use your knowledge and apply it in theoretical ways.

The Assessment and Qualifications Alliance (AQA) is an Awarding Body providing a Media Studies course that reflects your interests and experiences while at the same time developing your knowledge and awareness of key media areas and issues. What is more, the GCSE course is designed to flow smoothly into the AS and A Level courses for those of you who take the subject to a higher examination level.

Before you start any course of study it is always a good idea to have an overall idea of what that course will involve, what will be expected from you in terms of workload and assessment and what you will have to do to get the best possible grade. To do this you need to understand what **Key Concepts** and **Assessment Objectives** are and what role they play in your GCSE Media Studies for AQA course.

What are Key Concepts?

The Key Concepts form the basis of the subject content of your course. These are:

● Media Language: forms and conventions

● Audience

● Institutions

● Representation

You will study the Key Concepts in detail, but will find that they are not always separately presented – the course will allow you to look at how they work across different media text types, such as television and magazines.

● **Media Language** means the ways in which media texts communicate with people that use them. You may find out about camera movement, editing, and so on.

● **Audience** study turns attention on how people receive these communications. You may learn when studying popular music about how audiences are targeted by record companies, or about the way two papers present the same story when studying newspapers.

● **Institution** study turns your attention to the people who own and make the media texts people enjoy every day. If the area you are looking at is Film, you could find out about how films get to appear at your local cinema and about who decides what certificate they get. Institution in a radio context could be studied by finding out how news is gathered and produced at your local radio station.

● Studying **Representation** allows you the chance to see yourselves and others as the media see you and find out whether you still recognise yourselves. You might find out about the way people from your area of the country are presented on television or how people from different professions appear in films.

What will I be studying?

During your course you will be studying a wide range of media forms. The AQA course offers opportunities to study Television, Film, Radio, Popular Music, Newspapers, and Magazines and Comics: a selection that has something for everyone! You may study all of these, but you only have to cover three. Within these topic areas there are also opportunities to study advertising, cartoons and animation.

Whatever area you have been looking at, the work you will be asked to do will assess your ability to do three things:

1   To know about and understand the media texts you have been studying (known as *Knowledge and understanding*).

2   To analyse and interpret them – that is, think about how they work (known as *Analysis and interpretation*).

3   To make some media texts of your own by learning skills in production such as using cameras or software packages, as well as showing off your creative side by designing front cover pages for texts like fanzines (known as *Production skills*).

What are Assessment Objectives?

Assessment Objectives are the criteria that the Awarding Body, AQA, uses to assess your capabilities. GCSE Media Studies for AQA has three Assessment Objectives that require you to demonstrate:

● Knowledge and understanding (AO1)

● Analysis and interpretation (AO2)

● Production skills (AO3).

Your quality of written communication will also be assessed under Assessment Objectives AO1 and AO2.

How do I get my marks?

The AQA requires you to produce a coursework folder, which accounts for 50 per cent of your total marks, and to complete one written examination (known as the Controlled Test) at the end of your course, which accounts for the other 50 per cent.

What do I have to put in my coursework folder?

One of the great things about GCSE Media Studies is that the coursework you do will be interesting, relevant to *you* and really good fun. You will be creating totally original pieces of work that you can be proud of. There have been some students who have kept their Media Studies coursework to show at University interviews. You need to choose your best pieces in the two sections outlined below.

Section A: Assignments (25 per cent)

In this section you produce three assignments of about 700–800 words each or the equivalent in design and production work (this is much shorter than you realise, and you will probably need to do a few **drafts**). The assignments are equally weighted and at least one assignment must focus on Moving Image (unless the topic for the Controlled Test is Moving Image).

Each assignment should focus on a different *media text type* (for example, Film) and cover all three Assessment Objectives (which are explained above). Across the three assignments all four Key Concepts should be covered, though each individual assignment is likely to focus on only one or two of the four Key Concepts.

This piece of coursework is your opportunity to use your analytical skills and apply any specialist media terms or even theories that you have learned. The style of this piece is short, snappy and to the point.

Section B: Practical Production (25 per cent)

This section combines a polished, final draft media text/product, with the planning you put into the finished product and a supporting account. The length of your practical production will depend on its complexity, and your teacher will be able to advise you on this. The supporting account should be about 700–800 words long, and explains how you researched, planned and actually made your product with a specific audience in mind.

The production should cover all three Assessment Objectives (which are explained on page 10). You may work on your own, in pairs or in small groups (no more than four per group). As part of the submitted piece, you will need to produce all your pre-production work (such as research, scripts, storyboards, mock-ups and so on) that you used to help you plan your practical production. You will need to show a clear engagement with the *forms* and *conventions* of mass media texts, as well as a clear sense of *target audience* and *institutional* context.

The production itself should be as complete as possible, in terms of the technology that is available to you. However, you do not necessarily need to produce an entire **text**. For example, if individually you were creating a new magazine it would not be expected that you produce the entire magazine; the front cover, contents page and double-page feature for the magazine would be sufficient for assessment purposes. If you were doing the same assignment as part of a group you would need to submit a proportionate number of pages.

This piece of coursework is your opportunity to demonstrate your **research** skills, your ability to adapt and develop ideas and to plan a finished product with a **target audience** in mind. It is also your opportunity to show that you can respond to research by producing something original, using appropriate **technology** confidently and explaining all your decisions.

At the end of this book there are units containing ideas for AQA coursework pieces.

A word of warning

No assignment or practical production may cover the topic areas of the Controlled Test, the details of which follow.

What happens in the Controlled Test?

The Controlled Test is 3 hours long, carries 50 per cent of the course marks and tests all three Assessment Objectives (which are explained on page 9). The Controlled Test uses a case-study approach focusing on one main topic. There are a number of tasks on the test paper (usually four) and they will deal with one or more of the Key Concepts. During the Controlled Test, you will need to show an awareness of the historical context related to the given Controlled Test topic area.

You will be entered for either the Higher or Foundation Tier depending on your achievements in class and the standard of your coursework folder. Each test paper is based on the same topic area, though the actual tasks themselves will differ between Higher and Foundation tiers.

How does the Controlled Test work?

You will be given the test paper and any necessary materials shortly after the start of the summer term. You are then allowed to prepare the tasks that are outlined on the test paper. The Controlled Test is sat under supervised conditions, as for a formal examination, at times chosen by your school or college. The three-hour time allowance for the Controlled Test may be divided by your school or college into no more than two shorter sessions, but you will not be able to take the question papers or the answer booklets away with you between the sessions.

How should I prepare for the Controlled Test?

You should research the topic by:

- looking at a range of similar texts
- finding out how texts have changed over time by looking at non-contemporary texts
- drafting answers and noting how long you take to do each question.

What should I do during the Controlled Test?

During the test you should:

- allocate specific amounts of time for each question
- keep a careful eye on the clock
- make points, give examples and explanations based on specific texts
- refer to non-contemporary texts where applicable
- leave enough time to read through your answers.

Final thoughts

If, now that you have read the information above, you still have questions about the structure of your GCSE Media Studies course, you can ask your teacher or visit the AQA website. Your teacher may also show you past papers for the Controlled Test.

You won't regret choosing Media as a GCSE option. It will give you so many skills that will be useful long after you have closed your examination answer booklet and sat back in your chair in that exam hall with a satisfied sigh.

You will continue to be bombarded by media messages throughout your whole life, but with your GCSE qualification (and – who knows? – perhaps A Level too, one day) you will always have the ability to approach any text with a critical and analytical eye.

1 Film

In this unit you will find out:

- how films use narrative devices, such as flashback, and camera techniques to convey meaning
- how audiences classify films by recognising their genre characteristics
- how institutions and organisations promote and regulate films
- how women are represented in films and film posters.

TALKING POINT

- Start off with an instant survey. First each person should write down their two favourite and two least favourite films.
- Now combine your chosen films into two class lists. Do the same types of films – such as adventure, fantasy, science fiction, romantic comedy and Westerns – appear on both lists? Were the same types of films popular with both boys and girls?

Genre

Did you find that it was easy to say what types of films your favourites were? If so, it is because you already know a lot about **genre**. You can also probably tell, from a few seconds of a TV trailer or even from a poster, what genre a new film is likely to be, and you will have certain expectations as a result. What film genre do these three words suggest: *Saloon, Sheriff, Gunfight*? You probably thought 'Western' before you even read the second word! Media producers rely on your ability to recognise genre when they promote new films, to arouse interest, expectation and anticipation.

ACTIVITY 1

1 Work in pairs. Make a table like the one below to show the characteristics of four popular genres: Romantic comedy, Disney animation, Science fiction and Horror.

Genre	Typical setting	Typical characters	Typical plots	Typical props	Typical themes
Romantic comedy		Young man, young woman	They meet, hate each other, coincidences throw them together ...		

2 Now share your answers with another pair. Add any good ideas that you missed.

In film, exploring the ways in which **genre characteristics** are used to create style and appeal is very important. Films are often a complex mix of genres – known as *cross-genres* or *hybrid genres* – to attract the widest possible target **audience**. For example,

---

Toy Story (1995) seems to be a simple Disney animation aimed at children. However, it also uses the genre characteristics of:

- Science fiction – Buzz is a Space Ranger
- Westerns – Woody is a sheriff
- Adult comedy – the voices of Tom Hanks and Tim Allen deliver witty one-liners.

TIP

You can find out more about any of the films mentioned in this unit from Internet databases via Heinemann Hotlinks.

ACTIVITY 2

1   Look at the poster for *Mars Attacks!* (1996) in **1**. What genres are suggested in the poster?

2   Watch a range of film clips or film trailers. How soon can you identify what genre each one fits into, and if it demonstrates cross-genre (hybrid) characteristics? What audiences will each one attract?

1 Poster for *Mars Attacks!* (1996)

Science fiction

The roots of science fiction

Literary heritage

Science fiction is a genre that has at its heart some form of technology which is not yet possible, but which could be one day. Science fiction novels were popular long before film was even invented. Early sci-fi novels include *Twenty Thousand Leagues Under the Sea* by Jules Verne (1870) and *The Time Machine* (1895) by H G Wells.

Even earlier, Mary Shelley's *Frankenstein* was published in 1818 when she was only 21. It was the first horror/science fiction story written by a woman. It told the story of a scientist who discovers how to make a dead man live again, with terrible consequences.

Early sci-fi films

With fantastic worlds, strange technology and almost magical events, sci-fi novels offered rich material for early film-makers. Some, such as *Frankenstein*, have been made and re-made many times as film technology has developed and offered increasingly sophisticated and realistic effects.

If you asked a group of people to draw a representation of Frankenstein's monster everybody's images would probably be very similar. This is because they are familiar with the **film archetype** representation of the monster from the first ever Frankenstein film, made in 1933 with Boris Karloff playing the monster.

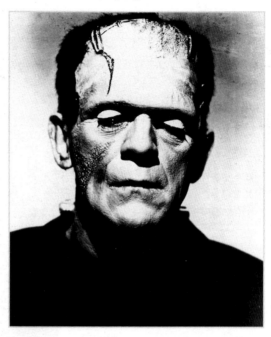

2 Boris Karloff as Frankenstein (1933)

The social symbol sci-fi

Because science-fiction narratives often include exploration, danger and new technology, they have been used to explore issues causing concern in society.

- The Frankenstein story was used in the 1933 film to explore the fear that men and women would become so taken up by factual scientific proof that they would stop believing in God.

- American sci-fi films in the 1950s and 1960s, such as *Dr Strangelove or: How I Learned To Stop Worrying And Love The Bomb* (1964), explored the fear that nuclear technology would result in the destruction of the world.

- *Invasion of the Bodysnatchers* (1956) seemed to be about an alien invasion, but was in fact about the McCarthy trials in the 1950s, when American citizens were questioned about their possible Communist sympathies.

> **ACTIVITY 3 EXTENSION**
>
> If you can watch *Invasion of the Bodysnatchers*, try to find out more about the McCarthy trials and then consider how the film relates to them.

The **blockbuster** sci-fi film

Until the early 1990s, sci-fi film was regarded as a minority genre which only longstanding fans watched. Then James Cameron produced special effects-driven *Terminator 2* in 1991, Steven Spielberg produced *Jurassic Park* in 1993 and Roland Emmerich wrote and directed *Stargate* in 1994. All these films were marketed to audiences as cross-genres of action with science fiction. With a big budget and special effects, Emmerich followed *Stargate* up in 1996 with *Independence Day*, and science fiction was established as a hugely exciting and action-packed genre for teenagers (**3**).

3 Sci-fi films became big hits in the 1990s

ACTIVITY 4

1 Find out as much as you can about the big blockbuster science-fiction films from the past few years. Which directors and stars have become associated with sci-fi films?

2 Which sci-fi films do you think most teenagers prefer? Can you explain why? Try to decide what the ingredients are that make a sci-fi film really popular.

Representations in science fiction

Representation is an important word in media studies. It means the ways in which people, places or events are *re–presented* to audiences. Representations of people are usually designed to make them as believable as possible, but if you look closely at representations of key social groups such as women, men, teenagers, ethnic groups, old people, etc. you will see that they are often quite **stereotypical**. Many teenage representations show them as being disrespectful, moody and selfish – this is obviously a very narrow view of teenagers.

KEY TERMS

Representation how people, places or events are represented or portrayed to audiences in media texts

Stereotypical showing groups of people in terms of certain shared and expected characteristics, e.g. showing women as nagging housewives

ACTIVITY 5

1 Look at a range of film clips in several genres. Try to identify different ways that people are represented.

2 Make a list to show how similar social groups (women, men, teenagers, ethnic groups, old people) are generally represented.

3 Try to suggest examples of representations that are *not* stereotypical but seem to be genuinely convincing and 'realistic'.

Propp suggested in the 1920s that every story had characters in certain roles: hero, heroine or princess, villain, donor or mentor and helper (see page 101 to find out more about these roles). Science fiction can represent groups of people in unusual ways by allowing them to fulfil unexpected roles in societies that are wholly invented.

Representations of women

Sci-fi has offered women real opportunities to be empowered and to break away from the more helpless 'princess' role. Ripley in Ridley Scott's *Alien* (1979) and Sarah Connor in *Terminator* (1984) were given lead roles who had real power and strength and were often responsible for pushing the **narrative** forward. It could be argued that such women play the hero role rather than the heroine.

ACTIVITY 6

In small groups, find out about some or all of these characters. Present your findings as a display of images with accompanying factfiles.

- Lara Croft in *Tomb Raider* (2001)
- Ripley in *Alien Resurrection* (1997)
- Princess Amidala in *Star Wars I* and *II* (1999 and 2002)
- Sarah Connor in *Terminator 2* (1991)
- Lyndsay in *The Abyss* (1989)
- Trinity in *Matrix* (1999)

Representations of aliens

One of the great conventions of sci-fi is the presence of some amazingly memorable aliens! Try jotting down as many as you can in one minute.

Sometimes taking 'human' form, sometimes robot, sometimes imaginative life-forms from other planets, aliens allow film-makers to explore different patterns of behaviour, language and customs. The essential thing about aliens is that they are *different* from us.

It is not hard to see that aliens are often used as a symbol for themes of belonging and being different. They can also be a way for film-makers to explore social problems, such as prejudice, in a subtle way.

ACTIVITY 7

1 Create your own alien. You can make it friendly or hostile, but you must label your design by pointing out key features that make it different from a human.

2 Extend your design by writing a paragraph describing how the alien responds to humans, and what would happen if it came to Earth.

KEY TERMS

Narrative a story or account

Stock character supporting character who is often quite stereotypical and whose job it is to help the lead characters, to be saved by them or to die

ACTIVITY 8 EXTENSION

Other frequent representations in sci-fi films are: *scientists*, **stock characters** and *captains* or other leadership figures. Choose one of these representations and analyse their roles in one or two films of your choice, sharing your findings with the class as a presentation or display.

Reading science-fiction films

Reading a film is similar to reading a book. First you must know the language, and then be able to work out what it means. Use this checklist to help you to look for the most important features in a sci-fi film:

- *Characters* (including aliens) will have clear roles and purposes in the narrative.

- *Costumes* are important – especially in future worlds.

- *Settings* are part of the created world and often involve **special effects**.

- *Colours* are important and are often symbolic, e.g. neon green often symbolises 'the alien'.

- *Soundtrack* is a vital clue to suggesting mood, theme and key moments.

- *Conventions* such as space, jargon, gadgets, weapons, etc. all build up the understanding of the narrative.

- *Special effects* may play a huge part – look out for animation, CGI (computer-generated imagery – see page 111), clever use of camera angles, action sequences.

KEY TERM

Special effects
exciting and dynamic visual or sound effects used to create impact in films

ACTIVITY 9

Practise your reading skills in science fiction. Watch clips from a range of sci-fi films. Make notes on the conventions, themes and characters as you go. Write your notes up as an essay or report.

ACTIVITY 10 EXTENSION

Prepare a more developed film brief (proposal), based around the following idea:

An exploration spaceship has gone missing without warning, and a crew must be sent to rescue them. Led by a female Captain and a male First Officer, the rescue ship is captured by an alien ship and taken to a new world where the inhabitants have very strange customs. The original exploration crew are also there, and the humans must work out a plan to escape and get back to Earth – but not without tragedy, love and an unexpected twist of fate before the end of the film.

1 Give your film a title and explain its meaning.
2 Cast the main parts and explain your choices.
3 Outline the narrative more fully, explaining all the interesting details.
4 Design the film poster.
5 If you are going to develop this work into a coursework piece, plan the promotion campaign for the film. This could include: storyboard or trailer, merchandise designs, soundtrack CD cover and DVD cover.

TIP

Keep your work from Activity 10 in your coursework folder.

Film flashback

When you look at any key area of film, it is always a good idea to understand its background. Look at the key features of film history in **4**. You can see how changing technologies and changing patterns of audience response have led to developments in the types of films that are made by film companies and enjoyed by audiences.

1896: First moving pictures were screened to audiences. They were very short and featured actual events happening, so they were called 'actualities'. Examples included *The Sneeze* and *The Kiss*.

Early 1900s: Films became longer and began to tell stories. Some even used special effects. A good example is *A Trip to the Moon* (1902) by Georges Méliès. Films were silent, with on-screen text.

Hollywood began to dominate film production by setting up powerful (and rich) film studios. This was known as the Studio System.

1927: The first 'talking' film – *The Jazz Singer* – was released, changing film production forever.

1930s: The first films to use Technicolour were produced. Two good examples were Oscar contenders *Gone with the Wind* and *The Wizard of Oz* in 1939.

1950s: The popularity of epic films resulted in screens being bigger – an early form of today's widescreen technology.

1977: *Star Wars IV: A New Hope* was the first film to use Dolby surround sound.

1983: *Tron* was the first film to use CGI (Computer Generated Imagery).

1999: *Star Wars I: The Phantom Menace* was the first film to be filmed mostly using digital cameras – which meant digital editing was used too.

21st century: Films today use many techniques to increase viewing pleasure: multi-layered sound systems, wrap-around screens, 3D screens (IMAX) and so on. The next step might be virtual reality cinema!

4 Film – a brief history

Looking at narratives

Tzvetan Todorov devised a way of analysing narratives according to the way they move forward through different stages. He suggested that many narratives, regardless of their genre, could be broken into specific stages for analysis.

Todorov's Narrative Stages

Equilibrium – the setting is established, key character(s) are introduced and the storyline is set up.

Disruption – oppositional character(s) appear and the story takes a particular direction.

Recognition of disruption – the lives of characters and events are interwoven. Tension builds throughout this section, which is often the longest.

Attempt to repair disruption – the highest point of tension after which there is a change in dynamic.

Reinstatement of equilibrium – matters are sorted out, problems are solved and questions answered.

Emily was sick of waiting around for a wimpy prince to come and ask for her hand in marriage, so she decided to find one for herself. She soon came upon a dragon who was singeing the top of a freckle-faced boy's head.

Being a resourceful princess, Emily set a trap for the dragon and then tricked him into following her.

'You're just a silly girl, and even though it's hardly worth it, I'm going to toast you to a crisp and have you for pudding!' boomed the dragon. Just then, the branches he was standing on gave way, and he fell down a very deep well, his fire put out once and for all.

Emily returned to the boy. 'What's your name?' she asked.

'Prince Matthew,' said the boy.

'That'll do nicely,' said Emily. 'Where do you live?'

'In Happy-Ever-After,' he replied.

'That'll do nicely too,' said Emily. And with that, she and Matthew rode off together to Happy-Ever-After.

5 Emily and the dragon

Why, you may well be asking, is the children's fairy story in **5** in a book on GCSE Media Studies? The answer is that the **narrative structure** suggested by Todorov fits this story so perfectly, and there are many useful activities arising from it.

ACTIVITY 11

1   Create your own chart to show how the theory can be applied to Emily's story. The first two sections have been done to help you.

Equilibrium:	We meet key character Emily, find out that she wants to find a prince for herself.
Disruption:	Emily meets oppositional characters: the dragon and boy.
Recognition of disruption:	
Attempt to repair:	
Reinstatement:	

2   Work in a small group to find each of the stages in two films you know well.

3   Watch a short narrative – a cartoon would be a good text to use. Analyse its narrative structure by breaking it down into its five stages.

4   Think of your own simple story featuring a small boy or girl. Write a 50-word story that follows this narrative structure and read it to a partner.

Playing with narratives

Obviously not all narratives fit into the linear progression suggested by Todorov, especially if they are trying to do something different or unpredictable. For example, in the film *Back To The Future* (1985) directed by Steven Spielberg, a boy travels back in time to meet the scientist who invented time travel. The stages of the narrative in this film are not in chronological order. Can you think of any other examples?

The correct term for something that does not fit a recognised theory is a **subversion.** You may recognise these subversion techniques:

● *Flashback* – where a section of the film is referred back to, e.g. *The Hulk* (2003) directed by Ang Lee.

● *Flashforward* – where a section of the film from the future is shown before it would normally have happened, e.g. *The Matrix Reloaded* (2003) directed by the Wachowski brothers.

● *Twist* – where part of the film (often the end) is unpredictable or even shocking, e.g. *The Sixth Sense* (1999) directed by M. Night Shyamalan.

● *Parallel narratives* – where the lives of characters move alongside each other for some of the film without them meeting, e.g. *Independence Day* (1996) directed by Roland Emmerich.

KEY TERMS

Narrative structure the way in which a story is organised and shaped in terms of time and events

Oppositional characters characters who will play opposite the key central character, either in a relationship, e.g. the hero/heroine, or in conflict, e.g. the hero/villain

Subversion when a technique is used which does not fit a theory or the usual way of doing something

ACTIVITY 12

Divide into groups. Look again at Emily's story in **5**. Each group should prepare to re-tell the story, using one or more subversions. Change the original version so that the narrative no longer follows the same path. The following suggestions may help you:

- Flashback – start the story from the moment when Emily is facing the dragon.
- Flashforward – begin the story with a dream sequence in which Emily faces a fire-breathing beast.
- Twist – Emily does not have to be human!
- Parallel narratives – tell Emily's story side by side with Prince Matthew's (or the dragon's) story. This could make the audience feel differently towards them.

Audience positioning

Audiences enjoy texts most when they are really involved in them. When you analyse a media text such as a film, identify the key techniques that 'sew' the audience into it. When they are genuinely hooked into the text's narrative and development, it is as if they actually have their own position in it. You can see why this is so important – someone who is really involved in a text is much less likely to switch it off or put it back on the shelf. Here are some techniques that help an audience to become involved or positioned in a film or television text.

- **Point-of-view shots** – the camera adopts the position of a character within the text. This can be an over-the-shoulder shot, looking at whatever the character is looking at, or a shot from the point of view of the character. This is particularly powerful when the character is experiencing a strong emotion – the viewer is more likely to feel their emotion when taking their point of view.

- **Reaction shots** – the camera moves to an extreme close-up of a character's face to show their reaction to something that has happened (see **6**: Eddie Murphy in *The Nutty Professor* (1996)).

6 Reading facial expression is crucial to understanding a character's reaction

- **Insert shots** – this technique gives the audience extra or privileged information that one or more characters may not yet know, for example in a two-set scene with two characters in different locations. The audience knows what is happening to each of them when the characters themselves do not.

- **Shot reverse shot** – the camera alternates between two characters to show their building relationship (whether positive or negative), often as a conversation is taking place between them. This is a very common technique in dramas where the inter-relationship between characters is very important. The camera acts as a third person in shot reverse shot, giving the audience the impression that they are turning their heads from one character to the other.

7 These three images demonstrate the shot reverse shot technique

ACTIVITY 13

1 Watch a series of film clips from different genres. Identify as many techniques of audience positioning as possible.

2 Using a still camera, create a series of shots which demonstrate each of the audience positioning techniques. Display them in your classroom with an imaginary narrative situation written underneath each one. You can see an example in **7**.

Additional camera terms and definitions

A great deal of time is spent on setting up every scene in a film. It is important to position the cameras in just the right way to capture on film exactly what the director wants the audience to see. In addition to the techniques mentioned already, here are some other camera shots that you will be able to identify in the films you study.

Camera term	What it means
Establishing shot	The camera is set far back to show or to emphasise setting or location rather than the subject
Slo-mo	A moment which is replayed very slowly
Pan shot	The camera moves horizontally, taking in all the details along the way
Tracking shot	The camera moves alongside characters either using a hand-held technique or smooth dolly tracks
Zoom	The camera focuses in on, or out from, a subject by using a telephoto lens
Mini cam	A tiny camera is placed in an unusual place for effect
Steadi-cam	A weighted camera is strapped to an operator to allow hand-held but controlled movement

TIP

Using a chart or table to present textual analysis will help you to keep under the word limit.

ACTIVITY 14 EXTENSION

Watch the first ten minutes of one of these films: *Star Wars IV: A New Hope* (1997), *The Truman Show* (1998) or *Saving Private Ryan* (1998). Look for evidence of genre characteristics, narrative structure, audience positioning and carefully set up camerawork. Present your findings as a table, chart, report or essay.

Intertextuality

Have you ever experienced the thrill of watching a film and recognising a reference to another film? This type of link between two texts is known as an **intertextual reference**. Do you recognise the phrases 'I'll be back' and 'shaken not stirred'? Where have you heard them? Can you think of other phrases which you have heard used intertextually in films or TV programmes?

Intertextual references can be visual as well. You can find a good example of this in *Toy Story 2* (1999). The toys are riding around Al's Toy Barn in a Barbie Tour guide car and Rex the dinosaur is running behind them, his reflection clearly seen in the wing mirror. This is an intertextual reference to the scene in *Jurassic Park* (1993) when the T-Rex can be seen in the wing mirror chasing the tour guide vehicle – in this case, with the intention of eating the passengers!

Another example is the Robin Hood scene in *Shrek* (2000) when Princess Fiona fights Robin Hood and his men; she fights in the same style as Trinity from *The Matrix* (1999).

The story of *Bridget Jones Diary* (2001) is full of intertextual references to Jane Austin's *Pride and Prejudice*, although the settings and the characters of the heroines could hardly be more different. The basic storyline is similar: girl meets and hates boy but after many mishaps realises his true worth and marries him. Among other references,

KEY TERM

Intertextual reference when one media text mimics or refers to another media text in a way that many consumers will recognise

the hero's surname is Darcy in both stories. In case anyone missed the point, Colin Firth, who had played Mr Darcy in the 1995 BBC mini-series of *Pride and Prejudice*, was cast as Mark Darcy in the film.

How films are promoted: film posters

Film posters: giving information

Film posters are hard to ignore – they are large, they are eye-catching and they are often intriguing. How well do they communicate information about the genre, characters and events in the films? Look at posters **8** to **11**, showing films featuring movie star Reese Witherspoon. What genre would you expect each film to be? In what different ways is Reese Witherspoon presented in these posters?

8 *Pleasantville* (1998)

9 *The Importance of Being Earnest* (2002)

10 *Fear* (1996)

11 *Election* (1999)

In pairs, use the information on the posters, both in words and pictures, to match these plot summaries to the film titles in posters **8** to **11**.

A Nicole discovers that her 'perfect' boyfriend David has a violent and disturbed side to his character.

B Jennifer and her brother David find themselves trapped in his favourite 1950s soap opera.

C This screen version of Oscar Wilde's play casts Reese as the young sweetheart Cecily in a comedy of manners.

D Tracy wants to be student president and uses some surprising tactics in this comedy film about the world of high-school politics.

Did you find lots of clues on the posters? Posters communicate information by the way the images are presented. The **gesture codes** of the characters instantly signal violent and disturbing events or romantic and comic moments. Other details, such as costume, location and lighting, also help us read the poster's messages.

A key message is the genre of the film. Next, the poster gives clues about the story in the **tag line**. Tag lines can become well known in their own right:

● The science fiction/horror classic *Alien* (1979) had the famous tag line *In space, no one can hear you scream ...*

● *Jaws 2* (1978) had the tag line *Just when you thought it was safe to go back in the water*. This was an intertextual reference to the first film *Jaws* (1975), which had been a huge hit. It reminds the audience of the terror of bathing in shark-infested waters.

ACTIVITY 16

Think of some catchy tag lines for these films:

● *First Victim*: a new monster, part werewolf, part vampire, hits town, looking for his first victim – a teenager.

● *No Way, Baby*: high-school heart-throb Jay is determined not to get tied down in a steady relationship. The high-school babes have other ideas!

● *Triple Deceit*: Detective Pacino is baffled by a series of murders until his new partner gives him some valuable insights. But where does she get her information?

Film posters: promoting stars

One way a poster can grab people's attention is to show pictures of the film's stars. The more popular the star, the more dominant their image will be in the poster. Stars are said to be 'A' or 'B' list depending on how popular they are. Can you identify the biggest **box-office draw** in each of posters **12** to **15**?

KEY TERMS

Box-office draw a performer whose popularity is likely to make a film successful; they are said to *carry* the film

Gesture code how a media text conveys a message using facial expression or body language

Tag line short, catchy statement on a film poster suggesting the film's content

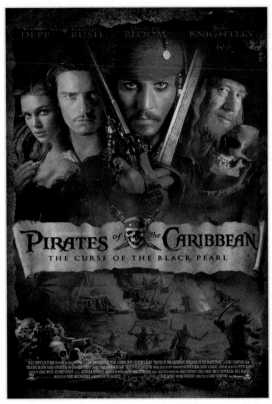

12 *Pirates of the Caribbean: The Curse of the Black Pearl* (2003)

13 *Titanic* (1997)

14 *Vanilla Sky* (2001)

15 *The Hours* (2002)

How could you tell who carried each film? The size and position of the star's name and image are so important that they are part of the star's contract for the film. Big stars try to get their name on the left of the poster and their picture on the right, because these are the most eye-catching positions. Who has these positions in **12**?

Posters are used to publicise and promote a film when it comes out in the cinema. They may be used again when it is available to rent or, a couple of months later, buy on video or DVD.

Film posters: targeting audiences

Film posters target audiences, and audiences in different parts of the world like different sorts of films. They may be particularly interested in a film set in their own country, and people of different cultures may find different types of films, or different features of the same film, appealing. Although the film remains the same, posters may portray it quite differently in different countries.

16 *Whale Rider* poster shown in the UK

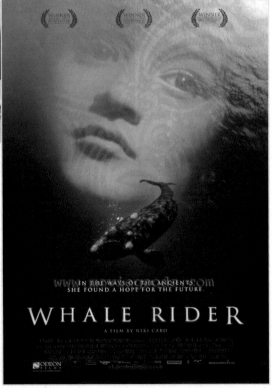

17 *Whale Rider* poster shown in the United States

Other ways to promote films

The poster works alongside other promotional techniques such as **newswraps**, magazine articles and newspaper articles, personal appearances by stars and directors on television, Internet advertising and items on news programmes to create interest in the film. These are seen particularly in the weeks before awards such as the Baftas and the Oscars.

Trailers

Trailers in the cinema and on television give viewers a taste of the film itself and are designed to have maximum impact. Trailers on TV last about 30 seconds and are usually for films expected to be blockbusters, which have much bigger publicity budgets than other films. Like posters, they promote the film to the general public.

The cinema trailer, on the other hand, can target a particular audience – filmgoers. In fact, the films trailed are often of a similar genre to the main feature, targeting the audience more precisely – they offer the audience something like the film they have paid to watch. Cinema trailers are longer than TV trailers, often lasting a couple of minutes, and several trailers are shown. Unlike TV trailers, they have a **captive audience** who are waiting to see a film they have paid for.

Trailers are usually made by specialist companies. They have certain common features in order to convey in a couple of minutes a message that people will remember. The best bits of the film are often shown, and codes are used to give information quickly.

● **Action codes** use one action to indicate what is going to happen: a character is seen taking down a suitcase, so you know that they are going on a journey.

KEY TERMS

Captive audience people who, for whatever reason, are unlikely to stop consuming a media text

Newswrap video compilation including clips from the film, interviews with the stars and/or director and other background material given to television companies to use when covering a newly released film

- **Enigma codes** set the scene while giving very little away. A hand is seen writing a threatening letter. Who is writing the letter? Why?

Trailers often leave the audience with a question that can only be answered by seeing the film.

TIP

You can find trailers to study on videos and DVDs of other films.

ACTIVITY 19

Watch some film trailers from a variety of different genres. In groups, list their features in a chart like the one below. How do these features make people want to see the film?

Genre	Features	How they make people want to see the film
Adventure	Action scenes Fast-moving vehicles Loud sound track Deep-voiced male voice-over	People know the film will be exciting People like to feel they are driving them Young people like loud music People feel safe – someone strong is in charge
Romantic comedy	Characters are good-looking and fashionable	People want to look like that

18 Still from the trailer to *Spider-man* (2002)

Premieres and festivals

Lavish film premieres often hit the front pages of newspapers, particularly if the star is a glamorous woman, bringing the film to the notice of non-filmgoers. Celebrity magazines such as *Hello* will give such events extensive coverage, boosting the profile of both the film and its stars.

A film may also be shown at a festival. There are lots of festivals to choose from and awards to aim for, but care must be taken. Sometimes films that are successful at festivals can be regarded as too arty and as having less popular appeal. There are international festivals at Utah, Berlin, Cannes, Toronto, Venice, Santa Monica and Milan. The UK's two main festivals are at Edinburgh and in London. These are aimed at public audiences and are well sponsored. They show the best of new cinema from around the world.

19 Film premieres promote films and also stars – Orlando Bloom and Liv Tyler at the premiere of *The Lord of the Rings*

Distribution

Distribution varies from film to film. Films with big budgets may, in Britain, start with release in big London cinemas and then go on **general release**. Less highly financed films will appear at selected cinemas. Some films never make it to the cinema and go 'straight to video', either because their quality is thought to be poor, or because there is no money to promote them.

Spending huge amounts of money on making and promoting a film expected to be a blockbuster is no guarantee of box-office success. There have been many expensive flops, for example *Waterworld* (1995), starring Kevin Costner, which was said to have cost over US $150 million to make, was disliked by the critics and not an immediate success with the public, although it is believed to have made money eventually.

There have been surprise successes too. The box-office success of *Romeo and Juliet* (1996), directed by Baz Luhrmann, was so unexpected that not enough prints of the film were available! One of its stars, Leonardo DiCaprio (**20**), became a box-office draw, appearing soon after in the film *Titanic* (1997), which won eleven Oscars.

20 Leonardo DiCaprio, a star of *Romeo and Juliet* (1996)

British film *The Full Monty* (1997) was a surprise hit for another reason. It was a low-budget film, so little money was spent on publicity and there was limited distribution. It proved to be a huge hit, mainly because people who saw it thought it was very funny and moving, and told their friends to go and see it. Before long, the film was packing out the cinemas all over Britain and it enjoyed success in the USA too. One of its stars, Mark Addy (**21**), appeared in several Hollywood films as a result.

21 Mark Addy appeared in low-budget film *The Full Monty* (1997)

Film classification

Before any film can be shown in the cinema or sold as a video or DVD, it must be assessed by a regulatory body to decide which age group it is suitable for. The BBFC classifies films, while the ITC grades videos and DVDs. You can see the BBFC classification scheme in **22**.

 Universal: suitable for everyone.

 Children under 12 can see the film only if accompanied by an adult.

 Video release particularly suitable for pre-school children.

 Not suitable for people under 15.

 Parental Guidance: anyone can see the film, although some material may be unsuitable for children.

 Not suitable for people under 18.

 Not suitable for children under 12.

 Video can only be sold through licensed sex shop.

22 The BBFC film classification scheme

UNIT SUMMARY

Key area	What you have learned
Media language	• What a narrative is. • How narrative is structured in stages. • How some narratives use subversions. • How modern films are often cross-genres. • The generic features of trailers.
Audiences	• How genre characteristics allow audiences to classify films. • How audiences are sewn into films to keep them interested and involved. • How film posters target national audiences.
Institutions and organisations	• How film companies promote films.
Representation	• How film posters represent women. • How science fiction films portray women and aliens.

2 Television

In this unit you will find out:

● how different television genres use codes and presentational devices to convey meaning
● how television attracts, retains and is used by its audience
● how the way a channel is funded affects the programmes that it shows
● how television programmes represent groups and individuals as stereotypes, and how these stereotypes change over time.

TALKING POINT

• When, how much and under what circumstances do you watch television?
• What would you miss most if you had to spend three months without it?

Television – a brief history

Did you find it hard to imagine life without television? Yet just sixty years ago it was unusual for a family to have even one black-and-white television set, let alone a colour, widescreen, surround-sound system in the living room and possibly another one in your bedroom! To get a good idea of the major developments in television history, look at the timeline in **1**.

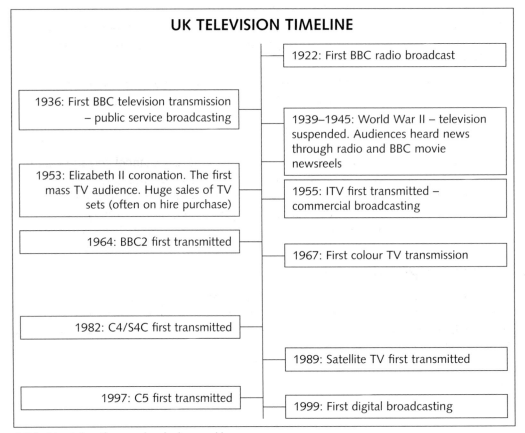

UK TELEVISION TIMELINE

1922: First BBC radio broadcast

1936: First BBC television transmission – public service broadcasting

1939–1945: World War II – television suspended. Audiences heard news through radio and BBC movie newsreels

1953: Elizabeth II coronation. The first mass TV audience. Huge sales of TV sets (often on hire purchase)

1955: ITV first transmitted – commercial broadcasting

1964: BBC2 first transmitted

1967: First colour TV transmission

1982: C4/S4C first transmitted

1989: Satellite TV first transmitted

1997: C5 first transmitted

1999: First digital broadcasting

1 Television is less than one hundred years old

KEY TERMS

Commercial broadcaster a channel funded by money from advertising

Peak time the hours between 6.00pm and 10.30pm when most people are watching television so that viewing figures are at their highest

Public service broadcaster a channel funded by a licence fee that has to provide a choice of programmes to appeal to all social groups

When the BBC first began transmitting radio programmes in the 1920s and television in the 1930s, it was as a **public service broadcaster.** This means that, in return for the payment of a licence fee, the BBC will provide viewers with a service of programmes that are guaranteed to 'inform, educate and entertain' and to appeal to as wide an audience as possible (this is known as the *public service remit*).

When ITV first began transmitting television programmes in the 1950s it was as a **commercial broadcaster** whose programmes are funded by advertising revenue. Independent TV channels are paid money in return for time slots that advertisers use to promote their products. Such time slots vary in price depending on whether they are during **peak time** (6.00pm to 10.30pm) or not. This is the time of day when audiences are at their greatest.

ACTIVITY 1

1 Conduct a class survey to find out which channels you watch most frequently. Each choose your top three favourites out of the following channels and award three marks to the first choice, two to the second and one to the third. Then add up the class marks for each channel.

- BBC1
- BBC2
- ITV1
- Channel 4/S4C
- Five
- Sky One
- Sky Sports channels
- Music channels
- Movie channels
- E4

2 Look at the television schedule for any day of the week in a TV listings magazine. Count up how many programmes on BBC1 and BBC2 are informative, educational and/or entertaining.

3 Now look at the programmes that are on the other channels listed above during peak time. Can you identify any types of programmes which are especially popular during peak time?

4 Discuss as a class or in small groups whether or not the BBC should be allowed to continue charging a licence fee. Use information from this activity and the class survey.

What do you think would happen to viewing choices if every channel was funded by advertising revenue? Advertisers are most interested in buying time slots around or during peak-time programmes, when most people are watching. This pressurises commercial broadcasting channels into producing more and more of the types of programmes that are most popular. Does this necessarily lead to quality programmes?

Television production

Television programmes are either made directly by television companies, or commissioned from smaller freelance companies. What are the factors that contribute to the making of successful programmes? Look at the list in box **2** – which components do you think are the most important?

A Key roles

- *Executive Producer* – arranges finance and oversees the whole project, including editorial decisions.

- *Producer/Director* – is responsible for the setting up and shooting of every scene.

- *Scriptwriter* – writes the script for the programme; this could be from an original idea or an adaptation.

- *Researcher* – ensures all details of location, sets, props and costume are appropriate and accurate for the style and time period of the programme.

- *Production Assistant* – looks after all administration, including scripts and running orders.

- *Locations Manager* – finds locations where a programme can be shot. Sometimes this will be a studio, but often a 'real' location such as a particular style of house or street must be found.

- *Camera Operator* – responsible for setting up every shot in a scene. This may involve working with other operators for techniques such as shot reverse shot.

- *Lighting Engineer* – works with Director and Camera Operator to ensure correct and safe lighting is provided on location or in the studio.

- *Sound Engineer* – ensures that different sound sources in a scene are balanced and that external factors such as wind do not interfere.

- *Editor* – takes the 'raw footage' shot each day and edits it into a sequence of scenes that tell the story. This can also involve adding music, fades and dissolves.

- *Costume Designer* – creates a set of costumes which are appropriate to the style and setting of the programme.

- *Make-up Artist* – ensures actors look right for their part; this can involve changing an actor in some way, e.g. by giving them realistic injuries in a medical drama.

- *Set Designer* – designs and builds sets that are appropriate to the style and setting of the programme.

- *Actors/Performers* – create believable characters.

B Stages of production

- *Pre-Production* – Ideas, bids for finance, storyboards, scriptwriting, planning and designing, set construction, casting, rehearsals.

- *Production* – Shooting in purpose-built sets or in outside locations.

- *Post-Production* – Editing, sound dubbing, credits, marketing and promotion, focus groups, trailers, articles and features.

2 Components of a TV production

The answer, of course, is that they are all important at different times and in different ways. Ultimately, it is the performance in front of the camera which attracts and keeps audiences, but for those performances to be outstanding, the team behind the camera need to have done their specialist jobs first.

A television production is a complex task, and planning is absolutely vital. However, some things are unpredictable, no matter how good the plan.

- Multiple takes are often needed to 'get it right' in front of the camera – look at programmes which are about moments when actors do not get it right.

- Live audiences: unpredictability on the part of guests and audiences and having to manage large numbers.

- The weather: some programmes have to be cancelled due to poor weather conditions, while others have to be suspended until weather conditions are right – it is not always possible to create a sunny day.

- Illness or scandal: a key character or presenter may be too ill to appear or involved in some public scandal.

- Special effects and stunts do not always go to plan.

Skill and teamwork are needed to get over these problems as they arise. Summer scenes for the *X-Files* were filmed in snowy Vancouver by blowing the snow off the grass first.

Title sequences

The language of the moving image text is a complex mixture of codes and messages that audiences are expert at reading and understanding. A great way to find out about the ways moving image texts communicate with audiences is by examining **title sequences**, which are highly crafted short texts.

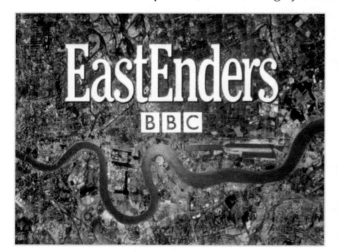

3 Images from the title sequence *of EastEnders*

Look at the shots in **3** from the title sequence of *EastEnders*. What clues do they give you about the programme? You can see some ideas in the table on the next page – can you add any to the list?

What you can see	What you can work out about the programme
The River Thames	It is set in London.
The Millennium Dome at Greenwich	It is set in the present, probably near Limehouse Reach.
The title is in big, bold writing.	It is called EastEnders.
The second image is in more close-up than the first.	The programme will focus on a small part of London.

If you are able to watch the opening, you will be able to pick out many more points. For example:

- The camera looks down on the map and rotates just before the title comes up, giving the viewer a different view of the river and its surroundings.

- The title emerges from the map just as the private lives of the characters emerge from their East End homes in the storylines for the programme.

> ## ACTIVITY 2
>
> Watch the title sequence of *Coronation Street*. Pick out the features that give you clues about the programme and put them in a table like the one for *EastEnders*.

Did the *EastEnders* title sequence tell you anything about the characters in the series? You may be surprised that no characters appear, but producers of title sequences often avoid showing people because then the sequence has to be changed much more often as characters join and leave the cast. The title sequence of *Neighbours*, for example, includes characters and has to be changed regularly. Look back at **3**: why do you think that the *EastEnders* sequence had to be changed in about 2000?

One way to approach the analysis of texts such as title sequences is to break down the task into three distinct areas, each of which focuses on a different type of code (see the diagram in **4**).

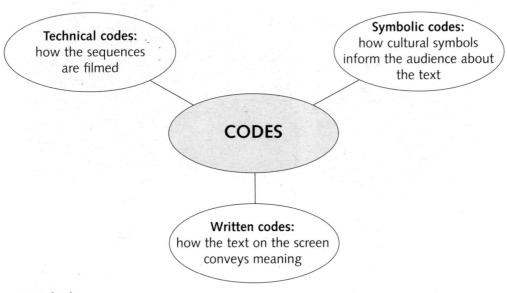

Technical codes: how the sequences are filmed

Symbolic codes: how cultural symbols inform the audience about the text

CODES

Written codes: how the text on the screen conveys meaning

4 Types of codes

> ### TIP
>
> Spider diagrams are a quick and clear way to show the examiner what you know.

KEY TERMS

Dissolve when one screen image fades into another

Fade when the screen image gradually disappears

Transition moving from one screen image to another

Wipe when one screen image appears to wipe away another

Technical codes

Technical codes include any of the technical processes used to create the text. Features to look for include:

- *Types of shot*, e.g. establishing shots. These may be of famous landmarks, such as the Millennium Dome, that indicate where events take place, or of signs to show where they are (see **5**) or what their function is, e.g. a sign saying Grange Hill School.

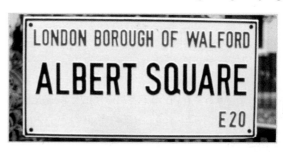

5 This establishing shot shows the location of *EastEnders*

- The **transitions** between shots, such as **fades**, **wipes**, **dissolves** and others.

- The *angle of the shot:* low angles make the subject seem larger and more imposing; high angles have the reverse effect.

- *Camera movements* such as *zooming in* on a subject or *tracking shots*, where the camera follows alongside the subject. This type of shot gets its name from the tracks that are put down so that the camera moves smoothly (**6**).

6 A camera recording a tracking shot

Symbolic codes

Objects, settings, body language, clothing, colour and soundtrack – the **mise-en-scene** of the sequence – use **symbolic codes** to inform the viewer. As you examine the text, you read the meaning of what you see and hear. People's cultural backgrounds will be important in the way they read an image. Facial expressions and body language are read according to the ways people's backgrounds have led them to interpret them. A polite hand gesture in some cultures may give offence in others. It all depends on a person's **situated culture**.

KEY TERMS

Mise-en-scene settings, costumes, body language, etc. used within the scene to convey the message to the audience

Situated culture the everyday surroundings and modes of behaviour shared with others from a similar cultural background

Symbolic codes how cultural symbols inform the audience about the text

7 What can you tell about the characters of *Neighbours* from these images?

ACTIVITY 3

Watch the title sequence of *Neighbours*.

1   Answer these questions using only what you can see.
   • Where do the characters live?
   • What is each of the characters telling us from their expressions and gestures?

2   Imagine you have been asked to introduce a new character into the programme, such as an elderly aunt who nags everyone. In groups, try different poses and facial expressions to suggest the sort of character you want. Act these out for the rest of the group as a 'freeze-frames' or tableaus where you adopt the pose and stay perfectly still to show what the still picture will look like. Discuss which was the most effective and appropriate for the programme.

If you watch the title sequence you will also hear the **signature tune.** This soon becomes recognisable to the audience and is seen as belonging to it like its 'signature'. Signature tunes signal themes in different ways.

- Some signature tunes communicate meaning through the style, mood and tone.
- Sometimes a particular instrument will be used to signal the setting. In *Coronation Street* the trumpet suggests brass band music associated with working-class northern England – the setting for the programme.
- Some signature tunes have song lyrics which prepare the audience for the programme by introducing themes that will be explored.

ACTIVITY 4

1 Think about the signature tune for *Neighbours*. What do the lyrics tell you about the story?

2 Choose one other signature tune with lyrics. How do the music and the words signal the themes of the programme?

Written codes

The writing on the screen may seem less important than the pictures and the music, but the font style and size, together with the position and movement of the text, can contribute to the ways the audience read the meaning. Look at the style of font used for the hit show *Buffy the Vampire Slayer* in **8**.

8 This lettering helps to convey meaning

Suggest two reasons why the title has been designed in this way. How does it signal the **genre** of the programme? Why has this particular font been chosen?

Does the font style make a difference to the way the text is read?

KEY TERMS

Genre a type or category of media text, such as a documentary, with certain predictable characteristics

Signature tune the soundtrack played over the images in the title sequence of the programme

Choose the best font from the box below for a title for each of these genres:

- Horror   • Romantic comedy   • Science fiction   • Game show   • Crime fiction

In each case the show is called *Last Chance*.

ALGERIAN	Fashion	MATISSE
Bauhaus	**Goudy heavyface**	**Matura Script Capitals**
Blackadder	*Jokerman*	Old English Text
Broadway	*Lucida Handwriting*	**Playbill**
Chiller	*Kendo*	**Serpentine**

If you prefer, find suitable fonts on a computer or design your own.

Case study: the title sequences to *Star Trek*

9 *Star Trek* was hugely popular in the 1960s

Sometimes the title sequence of a programme can become famous in its own right. In the 1960s the USA and Soviet Union were competing to put a man on the moon. *Star Trek* was first made in 1964 to exploit the interest in space travel this caused.

A voice-over was used in the title sequence to give the audience background information about the story. It explained that the crew of the star ship *Enterprise* were on a five-year mission to explore space – to 'seek out new life and new civilisations …' and 'boldly go where no man has gone before'. This phrase has become almost as famous as the series itself. Meanwhile the visual sequence showed the starship leaving the solar system and moving out into space.

Sequels used a similar title sequence, but changed 'no man' to 'no one'– what reason can you suggest for the change?

10 Later series of *Star Trek* kept the 'voyage of discovery' theme

Star Trek – the prequel

There have been many more *Star Trek* sequels, but when the title sequence to the **prequel** *Enterprise* (2001) was being designed new ideas were needed to give the show a different feel.

Enterprise is set 150 years after the present and 105 years before the original series. The early version of the starship *Enterprise* travels mainly in the solar system and is technologically behind the original and its sequels.

The title sequence abandons the usual style and instead shows a historical summary of human achievement in travel and discovery and human aspiration to travel in space. The ships shown in the sequence are all called *Enterprise* but they are not all starships.

The fictitious starships include the first warp ship, the *Phoenix*, as seen in the feature film *Star Trek: First Contact* (1996), and finally, the 'new' *Enterprise NX-01* that features in the series. Try to watch the sequence. At what point does the title sequence change from historical accuracy to fictitious events based on the *Star Trek* stories?

As well as changes to the overall visual style of the title sequence, *Enterprise* has a very different signature tune. Instead of the instrumental cue of the other series it has a contemporary soft-rock song called *Faith of the Heart*, performed by English opera tenor Russell Watson. The melody and the lyrics work alongside the pictures to suggest the past, present and future as well as the mission of Enterprise (both the series and the ship).

Media texts offer the audience a view of the world and sometimes invite them to make a judgement about events. How does the title sequence of *Enterprise* represent mankind's experience in terms of travel and discovery?

ACTIVITY 10

Look at the title sequences of the original *Star Trek* series, its sequels and prequels. How is human progress represented?

1 Watch a variety of title sequences. Comment on how meaning is conveyed through visual images and soundtrack. Consider:
   • how location and time are established
   • how groups of people are represented, if at all
   • how the soundtrack gives clues about the content of the programme
   • how any lettering used relates to the rest of the sequence.
2 **Storyboard** a title sequence of your own to launch a new programme (see pages 172–173 in Unit 9 if you need help). Think about all the features you looked out for in the sequences you watched.

Television genres

In media terms, a genre is any type of text – programme, film, popular music, etc. – that can be identified or recognised by typical conventions or characteristics (see pages 13–14).

1 Look in the daily TV schedule in a newspaper. List all the genres that you can find, such as situation comedy and news.
2 In small groups, think of a new TV programme aimed at teenagers. Write down what genre the programme belongs to and when it will be shown. Add any other important details, such as what will happen and who will feature in it.
3 Present your ideas to the rest of the class, and hear the ideas of other groups.
4 Think about all the ideas put forward. What were the most noticeable similarities and differences? Were there any particularly popular genres of programmes? Why might that be?

You will probably notice that some television genres are more popular than others, and that these are often scheduled during peak time. TV programmes are produced by teams of people who conduct extensive **market research** in order to find out what different audiences want to see on television. They are aware that audiences use the media to satisfy certain needs or requirements. Blumler and Katz discussed such audience demand in 1974 in their theory of Uses and Gratifications (see page 88). In summary, they suggested that audiences need to:

● be INFORMED and EDUCATED about the world

● IDENTIFY with characters and situations

● be ENTERTAINED

● use the media as a talking point for SOCIAL INTERACTION

● ESCAPE from their daily lives.

Look again at the television programmes and genres you identified in the daily schedules. Apply the Uses and Gratifications theory to them in order to see what audience needs are being satisfied by each genre. Put your answers in a table like the one below by writing ticks in the correct columns.

Programme	Inform	Identify	Entertain	Social interaction	Escape
Wildlife documentary	✓		✓	✓	

Introduction to television drama

Television drama is a hugely popular television genre, attracting wide-ranging audiences simply because there are so many different dramas to choose from in terms of both style and content. Since it is such a large genre, it is useful to divide it up further into **sub-genres** such as medical drama, police drama and docu-drama, in order to look at it more closely

11 David Jason in the Yorkshire Television drama *Micawber* (2002)

1 Watch the opening sequences of a range of TV dramas. Finish a copy of diagram **12** showing the typical sub-genre conventions or characteristics of each one. One has been done for you already. You may need to add more arms or boxes.

2 What other impressions do you get from the opening sequences? Try to add in more notes on your diagram about any of the following areas: *music, striking images, on-screen text*.

3 Discuss with a partner what storylines are suggested by the openings. What clues tell you the kinds of stories that will be important in the programmes? Look out for where the camera spends extra time, giving importance to certain moments and particular characters and their stories.

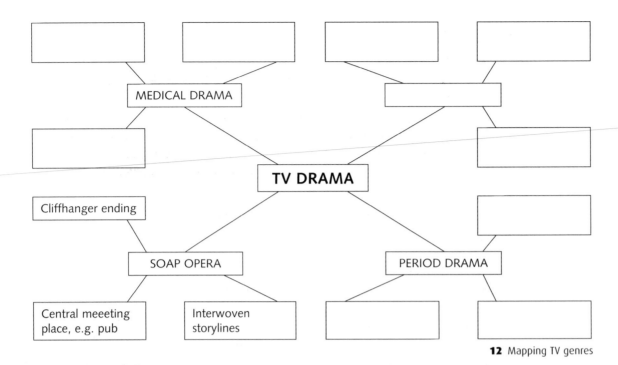

	MEDICAL DRAMA		

MEDICAL DRAMA

TV DRAMA

Cliffhanger ending

SOAP OPERA   PERIOD DRAMA

Central meeeting place, e.g. pub

Interwoven storylines

12 Mapping TV genres

Camera work

Some types of camera shots are used a lot in TV drama. The aim is to make it seem as though the audience is either 'there' in the scene through point-of-view shots or 'looking on' through the use of lots of close-ups and shots through windows and doors (see **13**).

13 A close-up from *The Bill*

Characters

Having central characters that the audience can get to know in lots of detail is absolutely essential to TV drama. These may play certain roles in the story, for example heroes, villains and helpers (see page 101).

ACTIVITY 15

Play a game with a partner.

1   Each of you should choose two characters from different well known TV drama series.

2   Think of three facts about each character and give them one by one to your partner as clues, starting with the most difficult to guess. Award 5 points for guessing with just one clue, 3 for two guesses and 1 for three guesses. (You could make this a whole-class activity with rounds and a final winner.)

Analysing character can revolve around several important areas:

● The character's role in the drama

● Their relationship with other characters

● The ways that the actor brings the character to life:
  – use of voice or accent
  – movement and gesture
  – emotional power to engage with the audience.

14 Characters in soap operas become very familiar to their audiences

KEY TERMS

Central protagonists key characters around whom the text and narrative are centred

Stereotypical grouping people together according to simple shared characteristics, without allowing for any individual uniqueness

The audience can usually spot two main types of characters in a drama – those who are less important and are there for 'padding', and those around whom the main narrative(s) centre. For example, in a medical drama the people who have accidents are only shown for some of one programme, whereas the hospital staff are seen week after week. The less important characters are less developed and often more **stereotypical** than the main characters or **central protagonists** (14).

ACTIVITY 16

Watch a clip from any TV drama. Decide which are the less important characters and which are the central protagonists. What information did you use to help you decide?

Setting

The location of a TV drama is important in establishing a sense of a real place where the story can exist. Many regional features may well appear, such as landmarks and the local accent, dress and customs of those who live there.

These features are included to encourage as strong a sense of engagement with the world of the drama, the characters and their lives as possible. Audiences continued to remember Dirty Den, for example, long after his exit from Albert Square because he was so perfectly set into the location and community of *EastEnders* – this also explains why his return was so well publicised. Fans of TV drama sometimes write in to their favourite characters, forgetting that they are played by actors and do not really exist.

One of the most important features of most television dramas is that they create believable or realistic worlds that audiences can watch and feel convinced by. The following case study will help you focus on just one sub-genre – the medical drama – in order to see how producers go about creating those real worlds.

Case study – medical drama

Medical drama is one of the most popular sub-genres of drama on television. It has its own set of conventions, all of which are designed to make viewers believe that the world of the programme really exists.

Medical drama developed from soap opera – serialised drama on radio and television paid for by washing powder manufacturers. It became clear that the audience for daytime soap operas – housewives at home during the day – also enjoyed dramas based in hospital wards and in doctors' surgeries. Before long soap operas appeared during peak-time viewing. Early examples included *Doctor Finlay's Casebook* and *Doctor Kildare*, which were extremely popular in the 1960s.

Two of the most popular UK medical dramas of recent years are *Casualty*, which began broadcasting on BBC1 in 1985, and its sister programme *Holby City*, also on BBC1, which began life in 1999. *ER*, on Channel 4, is an American medical drama set in Chicago that also has a large following (see **15**).

15 *ER* is a popular medical drama from the USA

KEY TERMS

Cross-plot a way of tracking different storylines through a single episode of a TV drama series

Multi-stranded narrative when a television drama not only follows more than one storyline but also interweaves them

Medical dramas often have a **multi-stranded narrative** where there is more than one story in one episode. The most important narrative in any particular episode usually acts as a cliff-hanger to keep audiences interested until the next episode. These narratives are interwoven or mixed together, and it is possible to draw a special chart called a **cross-plot** to make it easier to analyse how the narrative works.

Medics, 17 August 2004	scene 1	scene 2	scene 3	scene 4	scene 5	scene 6	scene 7	scene 8	scene 9	scene 10	scene 11	scene 12	scene 13	scene 14	scene 15
STORY 1 – Mr Singh Heart transplant	X		X		X		X		X	X	X		X		
STORY 2 – Mrs Spicer Heart harvest	X		X	X		X		X		X	X				X
STORY 3 – Paula The new job		X	*	X	*		*		*			X		X	

16 Cross-plot of an episode of a medical drama

Now that you have created your own cross-plot, you can analyse the ways in which the different storylines are interwoven, and how certain storylines dominate the episode. What do you notice about the pace and frequency of scenes towards the end of the episode? Which storyline does the episode end on?

Other important characteristics to look for when analysing medical drama are:

- a strong sense of realism in the setting and atmosphere
- a difference between the stable, regular characters (usually the doctors, nurses and medical personnel) and the visiting characters who are just there for one or two episodes (usually the patients and their relatives)
- sets that are carefully planned to be as believable as possible; décor, props and the behaviour of people in them are designed to convince the audience that they really do exist. Programme-makers usually have real doctors giving advice on the correct language and equipment to use in medical situations
- episodes that usually follow the pattern of a normal day, i.e. morning until night.

ACTIVITY 19

Watch two different medical dramas. Try to identify as many of the above characteristics as you can.

ACTIVITY 20 EXTENSION

Choose one popular British medical drama and one American one. Compare the storylines, characters and settings. Try to think of reasons to explain the main differences between them.

Medical cross-genres

You have already learned about the medical drama as a sub-genre of TV drama, but there are many cross-genres that have become very popular too. Examples include detective medical dramas such as *Diagnosis Murder*, crime thriller medical dramas such as *Silent Witness*, spoof medical dramas such as *Scrubs* and soap-style medical dramas such as *Doctors*.

ACTIVITY 21

1   Find two pages from TV listings magazines that have features on two different types of medical dramas.
2   Stick them onto A3 paper and label them, pointing out all their typical features and the ways the dramas have been made to seem interesting and appealing, e.g. by focusing on the dramatic developments in the storyline of a regular character to encourage viewers to want to see what happens to them.

Situation comedy

Types of humour

Think about your favourite sitcoms – you may enjoy them for all sorts of reasons, but above all it is because they make you laugh. Often the humour is based on visual comedy, like the classic 'pratfall' of the silent film era where the characters fall on their bottoms or slip on banana skins. This humour needs no explanation and works across different cultures because no language is involved.

Sometimes the humour is caused by the relationship between the characters – naughty children exasperating fathers or older brothers playing tricks on younger siblings. This comedy arises from the situation people are in, and is therefore called *situation comedy* or *sitcom*.

Humour also reflects people's beliefs and personalities, so they may prefer some programmes to others depending on their own experience.

Sitcoms and the family

The sitcom is now a television genre, but it began its life on radio in half-hour shows presenting characters in a common environment such as the workplace or the family home.

Family life has been a subject of sitcom since the early days of television. There have been many types of family represented. In the USA in the 1950s a hit sitcom *I Love Lucy* (**17**) brought to the screens a lovable yet hopeless housewife who was always getting into tricky situations that usually involved misunderstandings with her husband Ricky. The network did something unusual for the times with this live television show – they recorded it. This meant that they could show repeats and attract new audiences as the years went by.

17 Lucy and Ricky from *I Love Lucy*

ACTIVITY 23

1   Read this outline of an original *I Love Lucy* episode. How would Lucy and Ricky look and behave in a new series made for today's audiences? Think about the social changes that have taken place over the past fifty years, especially in the roles of men and women. Suggest ways to bring it up to date and think of comic complications that could happen before all is put right in the end.

> **Men Are Messy**
> Tired of cleaning up after Ricky, Lucy divides the apartment into two. He can mess up his half if he wants, but he cannot come into her half.

2   In groups, improvise some of the situations you have thought of. Vote for which you think would work best as an episode of a sitcom.

Although the types of things that go wrong that are the source of humour have not changed over time, other things have. One of the changes in society since the 1950s is that few women now are full-time housewives. Many of the plots of the *I Love Lucy* shows centred on her attempts to gain some independence, suggesting that her husband was very much the boss.

Plots in modern sitcoms still feature the battle of the sexes, but are the women stronger or weaker than the men? Read the article about the British sitcom *My Family* in **18**.

TIP

You can find out more about *My Family* by following the links on Heinemann Hotlinks.

Ben is the harassed centre of the Harper family. His wife Susan is intelligent, sharp, witty and something of a control freak, and their still-loving marriage is a vehicle that may squeak but nonetheless keeps moving along. Ben – though he complains a lot – knows that he has done well in this regard. Susan works as a tour guide, Ben as a dentist, and their home life is complicated by the normal wear and tear of three children. Nick, the eldest, is a lazy, slow-witted incompetent who nonetheless has a certain charm. Janey is a stereotypical teenager, concerned with boys, fashion and looks. Michael is the youngest, a serious, studious boy arguably brighter than his brother and sister. At work, Ben is assisted by his dense hygienist Brigitte (series one) and by son Nick (series two). Janey left to go to university at the start of the third series and returned at Christmas to announce that she was pregnant.

18 *My Family*

ACTIVITY 24

Discuss these questions with a partner.

1 What do you learn about each family member in the article?

2 Which characters, from their descriptions, do you think have the most power in the Harper household?

3 What kinds of conflicts do you expect between members of the Harper family from what you have learned about their characters?

4 Why do you think sitcom is so often based on family life?

The **representation** of men, women and teenagers in sitcoms is often stereotypical.

● Men are often seen to be weaker than their female counterparts, usually their wives. They may think that they are going to get one over on them, may even look as though they are going to come out on top, but they never win and end up either losing face or losing money.

● The women are often strong characters who keep the whole family on track despite the antics of their hopeless husbands and naughty children.

Do these stereotypes also apply to sitcoms from America? The USA sitcom called *Malcolm in the Middle* also explores what life is like in a family. The narrative style, or the way the story is told, centres on the Malcolm of the title. Read his description of the family as he sees them in **19**.

ACTIVITY 25

1 What similarities are there between the families in *Malcolm in the Middle* and *My Family*?

2 Work together in groups to produce a storyline for Malcolm and his family. Write the first two minutes as a monologue for Malcolm in the style of his journal as below.

My dad's a thinker – none of us knows what about! What my mum says, goes – she's in charge of everything, even the remote control. Francis, my oldest brother, is cool – so he got kicked out. Reese, the next, is dumb, dumb, dumb. And Dewey, the youngest, was only fun until he could talk well enough to tell tales. As for me, Malcolm – well, my skin is clearing up, Reese is in high school so I don't see much of him, and life is getting better – I think!

19 *Malcolm in the Middle*

The strong mother and the exasperated father are represented here in a family situation. The family seem less middle-class than the Harpers, less wealthy and even more dysfunctional, that is, it has difficulty functioning and communicating in emotionally healthy ways.

One of the reasons for the programme's popularity was its ability to present material the audience could identify with. Everyone likes to think their family is perfect, but also knows deep down that it is not, so it is reassuring to see families on television trying to work through problems, as everyone has to do. Could it be that this type of text offers its audience a way of dealing with feelings about their concerns and fears?

Grumpy old men

Another frequent sitcom stereotype is the 'grumpy old man'. Examples from the past include the father in *Steptoe and Son* and Alf Garnett in *Till Death Us Do Part*. More recent texts include *Phoenix Nights*, *Last of the Summer Wine* and US sitcom *Becker*. How many more examples can you think of?

It could be said that in the past comedy was a way for women and children to deal with the authoritarian husband and father figure in many families. The 'grumpy old man' was not only a figure of fun, but often ultimately powerless, as behind his back his seemingly downtrodden wife quietly got her own way. Do modern sitcoms portray this situation in quite the same way? Can you think of any recent sitcoms where the 'grumpy' or 'bossy' role is filled by a woman or a young person? For example, Patty and Selma in *The Simpsons* are both grumpy. What does this say about the changes in family structure?

20 Grumpiest of them all? Victor Meldrew from *One Foot in the Grave*

ACTIVITY 26 EXTENSION

In groups, research the use of the stereotype of the grumpy old man in TV sitcom in the past 30 years. Your research resources could include the Internet, TV listings, books and interviews with older relatives about their favourite grumpy characters. Present your ideas visually and in writing for a wall display.

Television news

Where do news stories come from?

Every story and item of news that you see on television has a source. Journalists have various sources for their stories:

- *Reporters:* Independent Television News (ITN) employs reporters in London and Westminster, with more in Manchester, Belfast, Cardiff and Southampton. They also have reporters based in Brussels, Washington, Bangkok, Johannesburg and Moscow.

- *Processed news:* this comes in the form of press releases.

- *Freelance journalists* may approach a station with a story, or may be commissioned to research one.

- *Foreign TV, the national press and radio* all provide stories. Stories from local television stations and newspapers sometimes appear on national TV news.

- *News Agencies* such as The Press Association and Reuters Association Press supply news from all over the world.

How are news items chosen?

With so many sources of news, there are far more stories than can be shown. *News at Ten* has a large audience who have many different interests. Football stories can and do make the headlines, as do items about popular television. Political stories are often considered to be more serious, but may not be as interesting to some sections of the audience. Those who select the news have to consider the whole audience and provide news which has relevance to the **mass audience**.

21 The news has to appeal to an audience with many different interests

ACTIVITY 27

It is your job to choose the four leading stories for tonight's ITN *News at Ten* from the items in the first column of the table below. At this stage, ignore the information about pictures. In pairs, select the items you think should make it into the headlines and put them in order – most important first.

Headline	Film footage available
Prime Minister apologises to Parliament for giving them incorrect information	Pictures of Prime Minister leaving 10 Downing Street and getting into a car
Missing girl – man arrested on suspicion of murder	Archive footage of suspect interviewed when girl first went missing six months ago
Arsenal sign striker from Real Madrid	Striker at press conference and attending film premiere with celebrity girlfriend
Plane crash in Bolivia	Dramatic footage of plane crashing into the sea plus eyewitness interview with crew member of aircraft carrier
Government introduces new initiative to help stop bullying in schools	Pictures of pupils in classroom (library)
Coronation Street to finish in the New Year	Pictures of demolition equipment moving into the set of *Coronation Street*
National Lottery to stop supporting charity to increase jackpots	Pictures of various charity projects that have received lottery grants

Which did you select? When you were discussing which of these stories to include, you probably asked yourself about the importance of the stories to the audience who watch the programme, deciding on the basis of their **news values.**

Galtung and Ruge suggested in 1973 that journalists considered these factors when they decided what was newsworthy:

- *Surprise:* was the event unexpected?

- *Frequency:* do these types of events happen often?

- *Elite nations and people:* does the event involve powerful countries or famous people?

- *Immediacy:* has the event just happened?

- *Personalisation:* is it a human interest story?

This process of selecting and rejecting is called **gatekeeping**. The gatekeepers who make the decisions will be influenced by their own backgrounds and education.

There are other factors that affect the selection of news for television in particular.

- *Did the station have a reporter on the scene?* Stations prefer to present their own unique footage.

- *Length:* Television news can only overrun for major events like the attack on the World Trade Center in September 2001.

KEY TERMS

Gatekeeping selecting and rejecting news items

News values the criteria journalists use to decide which stories are most newsworthy

- *Taste and decency:* Because television appears in the corner of family living rooms, there are particular constraints about what can be shown. News bulletins before the nine o'clock **watershed** must not show material unsuitable for children. Even after this time there are limits on the level of violence that can be shown. The rules that apply to news are stricter than those that apply to other programmes because real people are involved. People's feelings must be considered: a few days after the 9/11 attacks, networks agreed not to show the footage of the planes hitting the towers again, out of respect for those who had died and their families.

- *Are there are any good pictures?* Television is a visual medium and news stories are presented in both pictures and words. If you think about the news stories that have had most impact on you, you will realise that they are the ones that had the most dramatic pictures. News values can be distorted by availability of pictures. A story may not be used if there are no pictures. Pictures can sometimes be found from previous reports. When these are shown, the words 'Library Pictures' appear on the screen.

ACTIVITY 28

Think about your selection in Activity 27 again, this time looking at the information about the pictures. Decide if your choice of stories and running order has changed. Give reasons for your decisions.

ACTIVITY 29

Imagine you are a television journalist covering a news story at your school or college.

1   Decide on a possible story from this list:
    - The Head of Media Studies has been running a photography business on school premises.
    - It has been claimed that criminals have been selling illegal substances on school grounds.
    - The Head has been kidnapped and is held inside the building. Police are negotiating with the kidnappers.

2   How would you make sure that you presented a report that is unbiased and fair to the people involved?

3   What pictures would you try to capture to help you put together an interesting story?

4   Try writing up the text for the story. You may invent names and details. It should be three or four sentences long, 45–50 words in total (15 seconds speaking time at three words per second).

5   Now try out your newscasting skills. Have a go at presenting your story to the person next to you.

Television journalists may have to reject stories if they are in some way unsuitable. Here are ten questions that may be asked before a story is run:

- Is the story untrue or unconfirmed?
- Does it intrude on the privacy of a person or persons?
- Might it lead to legal action?
- Is it old news?
- Do other news channels have it?
- Is bad or blasphemous language used in the visual footage?
- Are dead bodies shown?
- Are executions shown?
- Are the details too violent or sexually explicit?
- Will it give offence to racial, religious, gender or disability groups?

ACTIVITY 30

Will these stories reach people in their living rooms? You decide! Give each of these stories the ten-question treatment.

A One of the royal children is rumoured to have cheated during an examination – information comes from a tip-off, probably from a schoolmate.

B More details on yesterday's story about fashion giants to close 100 stores with loss of many jobs.

C England captain swears at manager and says he fixes matches for money. Filmed interview with manager who denies allegations.

D Politician's wife involved in fraud – source is 'friend of the family'.

E Amateur video of police assault on two youths.

F Matador gored by bull in Spain.

Some news programmes like to finish on a lighter note because a lot of news is bad news. The type of story run at the end is often a sentimental account about animals – always popular with the British public. Journalists call this type of story a 'dead donkey', and it is the first story to be dropped if more exciting news breaks.

Different styles of news programmes

News programmes have the same features as other television programmes.

- *Sets* are designed to relate to the tone of the programme – the mise-en-scene is carefully chosen. Where the intention is to give the impression of a working newsroom, the presenters sit in front of a glass screen, as in **22**. Behind it, journalists are shown in an office, taking calls and writing stories using computers. If the intention is to make the programme more serious, the background is superimposed on a screen behind the presenter using **blue-screen technology**. This allows the images to look as if they are part of the set.

TIP

Keep a notebook of stories that hit the headlines for a week. You can use this to give specific examples in your coursework.

22 A television newsroom

KEY TERMS

Blue-screen technology the presenter (who must not wear blue) reads the news in front of a blue background, which is later digitally replaced by another backdrop. This is also known as *chromakey* or *colour separation overlap*; in some cases green is used.

Mode of address style of delivery adopted by presenters, which will depend on the audience and the tone of the programme

In less formal news programmes, often for younger audiences, the presenter leans on the desk while making the broadcast. Whatever the style, it has been deliberately planned in order to set the tone for the target audience.

● The *signature tune* for the programme also identifies the tone of the piece. Some bulletins have light, rising melodies; others are deeper and use drums and bass notes to create a more serious tone and lend the programme a degree of formality and dignity, making it seem important and truthful.

● The news has its own stars, newscasters also called *anchor men* and *women* because of their role in linking separate items together, in some ways like the presenters of a magazine programme. They will adopt a suitable **mode of address** for the audience and also the news item they are reading. In a programme like *Newsnight*, broadcast on BBC2, the anchors lead debates and conduct interviews as well as reading news bulletins.

● News programmes can have *catchphrases*. *News at Ten* presenters introduce the last item, which may be lighter in tone and content than previous reports, with the words: *And finally ...* This signals to the audience both the final item and the change of mood.

ACTIVITY 31

1   Think about the differences between the presentation styles and contents of news bulletins on BBC1 and Channel 4. Decide who you think is the intended audience for each. Try preparing a news item on problems in schools to be presented on each channel, making clear by the style and approach that you have understood the difference between them.

2   Are there particular types of people who read the news? Look at a variety of news programmes and note the ages, ethnic/regional background, accent or dialects, style of dress, etc. of the presenters. Is there any sort of person you would consider unsuitable to be a newsreader? Write up your findings as a report.

UNIT SUMMARY

Key area	What you have learned
Media language	• To use the theory of Uses and Gratifications • How meaning is conveyed through technical, symbolic and written codes • Understanding genre through case studies
Audiences	• How audiences gain pleasure from texts • How audiences are researched • How audiences understand scheduling
Institutions and organisations	• Who does what in the making of a television programme • How television has developed over time • The difference between public service and commercial broadcasting • How organisations such as news agencies influence what appears on news programmes
Representation	• How characters are created in television programmes • How characters in sitcoms can be stereotypical • The representation of reality

3 Newspapers

In this unit you will find out:

- how newspapers use codes and conventions to present the news
- how audiences are targeted and retained by newspapers
- how the content of a newspaper is influenced both by the institutions or organisations that own it and by those that provide news stories
- how the representation of individuals and groups in a newspaper depends on its viewpoint.

TALKING POINT

- Where can people find news apart from in newspapers? Make a list.
- Which is the main way that members of your families get their news?
- Look at a selection of newspapers. Suggest why people buy newspapers as well as getting their news from the sources you listed.

Why study newspapers?

Despite competition from TV, radio and the Internet, there is still no sign that, 300 years after the first newspaper was produced, a printed daily newspaper is a thing of the past. Thirteen million newspapers are sold in the UK every day: why do people read newspapers?

A recent survey asked adults aged 16–34 which words they associated with each of radio, television and newspapers.

- Newspapers were thought to be 'informative', 'serious' and 'influential' by more people than radio and television.

- Forty-two per cent agreed that 'newspapers are an important part of daily life'.

It is important for you to study newspapers as part of your GCSE Media Studies course – lots of people read them and lots of people think they are important. Before radio and then television were available, newspapers were people's main source of information about what was happening. You can see in **2** how the press in Britain has grown and developed since those early days.

1 This photograph appeared in *The Illustrated London News* in 1892. It shows the Duke of York (later King George V) and other officers on board *HMS Melampus*

A Brief History of the British Press

1702 First daily paper *Daily Courant* founded (last published in 1735).

1785 *The Times* is first published: UK's oldest surviving daily newspaper.

1791 *Observer* founded: UK's oldest surviving Sunday newspaper.

1806 First use of illustration in the *Times*: Admiral Lord Nelson's funeral.

1832 First recorded British newspaper cartoon, published in *Bell's New Weekly Messenger*.

1844 First story based on telegraphed news printed in the *Times*: birth of a son to Queen Victoria at Windsor.

1855 Repeal of the Stamp Act opens the way for cheap, mass-circulation newspapers and modern newspaper design, using spacing and headlines.

1889 Early use of photographs: Cambridge and Oxford boat crews, in *Illustrated London News*.

1900 *Daily Express* launched: first national daily to put news on the front page.

1903 *Daily Mirror* launched: first daily illustrated exclusively with photographs.

1963 *Sunday Times* launches a magazine-style colour supplement.

1987 First women editors of national newspapers in modern times: Wendy Henry (*News of the World*) and Eve Pollard (*Sunday Mirror*).

1991 Press Complaints Commission replaces the Press Council for more effective press self-regulation.

1994 *Electronic Telegraph* launched: first British national on the Internet.

1999 *Metro* launched: a daily newspaper distributed free to travellers on the London Underground.

2003 Some broadsheets go **tabloid**: *The Times* and *The Independent* publish a tabloid version in addition to their usual **broadsheets**.

2 The history of newspapers in the UK

3 *The Times,* 1 January 1788

Press freedom and responsibility

Not only in the UK are newspapers an important part of daily life – read the story by Andrew Meldrum in Pretoria about the Zimbabwean *Daily News* in **4**.

Zimbabwe faces intensified isolation by the international community after the Mugabe government closed the country's only independent daily newspaper.

Armed police stormed the offices and printing press of the *Daily News*, the country's largest circulation newspaper, late on Friday night to prevent it from publishing yesterday.

'We have been closed down. This is an unprecedented attack on press freedom,' said Francis Mdlongwa, the paper's editor-in-chief. 'We know that Zimbabwe is collapsing and that there's an attack on independent institutions but we never thought that they would go this far. This is totally unacceptable.'

4 Taken from
The Observer,
14 September 2003

ACTIVITY 1

In pairs or groups, discuss the following points:

- Why do you think the Zimbabwean government would want to close down the largest newspaper in the country?

- Should newspapers be allowed complete freedom to publish anything they want about the government of their country? Give reasons for your views.

- Do newspapers have the right to publish articles about the private lives of individual citizens? Are some people fair targets for having their lives spread all over the front pages? Why?

TIP

Find out more about press self-regulation in the UK from the Press Complaints Commission website via the Heinemann Hotlinks site.

UK newspapers

Daily newspapers – take your pick!

There are hundreds of different newspapers hitting the streets every day of the week in the UK. How many daily papers can you name? Look at diagram **5** for some ideas. The content and layout of each paper will reflect its **target readership**. The ten largest national daily papers divide into two categories: the *tabloid* or 'popular' papers and the *broadsheet* or 'quality' papers.

Tabloids

The five daily tabloids can be subdivided into two groups. *The Sun*, *Mirror* and *Daily Star* are called the **red tops** because they have red **mastheads**. These papers report on politics and international news but generally include more gossip about celebrities from the pop or film world and sleaze or scandal of any sort. Stories are written simply and are quite short. Red tops tend to have more pictures than other papers, particularly the broadsheets. Their main aim is to be an easy read.

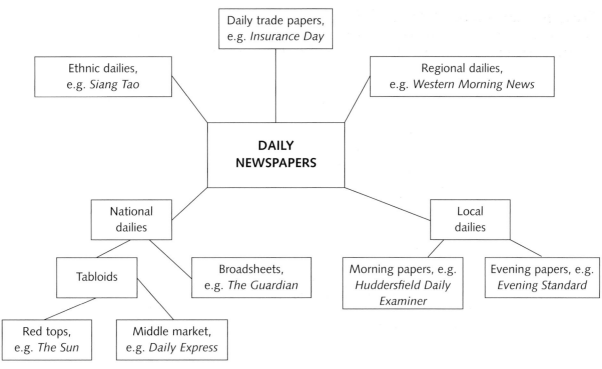

5 Daily newspapers in the UK

The *Daily Mail* and the *Daily Express* are often called the 'middle market' dailies. They target a readership somewhere between those of the red tops and the broadsheets. They print plenty of news and features for people wanting a paper that is not too gossipy or trivial, but they also have a variety of lightweight articles and pictures.

As well as entertaining, the tabloid papers line up behind one of the two major political parties. At one time only the *Mirror* was a Labour-supporting tabloid. In 1992, the Labour party were widely expected to win the General Election. But after John Major's surprise victory for the Tories, *The Sun*, which had supported the Conservatives, claimed that it had won the election for them. An important triumph for the Labour Party was to convince Rupert Murdoch, the owner of *The Sun* (as well as *The Times*, *The Sunday Times* and *The News of the World*) to change sides and back Labour. Five years later Labour romped home to a big victory – and the *Sun* could claim to have swung the election again.

Broadsheets

The five quality papers have higher news content, usually higher prices for each copy and lower circulation figures than the tabloids.

The Times is the oldest of all the dailies; it used to have the reputation for being rather stuffy and the 'voice of the ruling classes'. Right up until 1966 it had no news on its front page, just small advertisements and announcements.

In 1979 there was a huge dispute between the paper's owners and the trade unions about ways of modernising the paper's production, and the paper was closed for a year. It was then bought by Rupert Murdoch's News International company and is now a genuinely modern paper – it was only the second broadsheet to issue a tabloid version, in November 2003.

The Daily Telegraph is the broadsheet with the highest circulation. It is a very strong supporter of the Conservative Party. Its high circulation allows it to charge higher prices to advertisers; it generally carries more advertisements than the other broadsheets.

The Guardian started out as the *Manchester Guardian*, a regional paper for the north of England. Because it always supported left-wing political views it had a readership across the country. In 1959 it moved its operation to London and became a fully national daily.

The Independent is the newest of the national dailies, set up in 1986 and intended to be independent of any one political party's viewpoint. It also introduced different styles of layout and used more photographs than its competitors. In 2003 the paper issued a tabloid version as well as the broadsheet.

The Financial Times is the only national daily to be printed on pink paper. It reports mainly on business and economic news, although it does have other news, including a sports section.

Although the broadsheets have taken on more and more features from tabloid production, such as the use of very large photographs on the front page, there is still one major difference – the style in which the articles are written.

ACTIVITY 2

Choose one tabloid newspaper and one broadsheet. Work out the average number of words used in one sentence from each of the papers by picking ten sentences from different parts of the paper. Check your averages with those of a partner. What differences do you notice? Can you suggest reasons for these differences?

Ethnic newspapers

As Britain has become home to an increasingly rich and diverse number of cultures, a variety of newspapers have sprung up to serve this new market. Most are weekly or monthly publications but some are dailies, for example the *Caribbean Times*, the *Asian Times*, the *Daily Jang*, which is published in both Urdu and English, the Chinese *Siang Tao* and *Al Arab*. This area of the market has now developed to the point where take-overs and mergers are starting to happen. In January 2004, *The Times* reported that *The Voice* (circulation 30 000; target audience black Caribbean) was up for sale, probably to *New Nation* (circulation 35 000; Asian-owned) and may become one publication.

6 *Asian Xpress* is a successful Asian-owned daily

Local papers

Nearly a hundred daily local papers are published, mostly evening papers although there are nineteen morning titles. More people read local papers than national papers. Some estimates put readership of local papers as high as nine out of ten adults. Research suggests that people skim through national papers but read local papers much more thoroughly.

As well as often covering major national news stories, local papers offer stories about their readers' own community. These range from campaigning stories, about building a bypass or better bus transport, to reports of primary school carol concerts. They also carry pages of **classified advertisements** at the back of the paper. Except for those placed by Estate Agents selling houses, most classified advertisements do not have pictures. Research shows that people turn first to the local paper when they want to buy second-hand items, find a local tradesman or have their car serviced.

ACTIVITY 3

1   Conduct your own research into the readership of your local paper. Ask a cross-section of 25 adults the following questions:
    • Do you ever read your local paper?
    • How often do you read it?
    • How long do you spend reading each copy?
    • Which sections do you spend most time reading?
    • Do you ever use the classified advertisements?

    Do your results match the claim that most adults read a local paper?

2   Compare your results with those of a partner. Are there any differences in your findings? If so, what might be the reason for the differences?

The Sundays

The Sunday papers can be categorised in pretty much the same way as the dailies. At the popular end of the market are the *Sunday Sport*, *Sunday Mirror*, *The People* and the paper with by far the largest circulation, the *News of the World*. Over 40 per cent of all British adults are said to read the *News of the World*.

Both middle-market tabloids also print a Sunday paper – the *Mail on Sunday* and the *Sunday Express*.

All the broadsheets except the *Financial Times* have sister Sunday papers. Like *The Guardian*, *The Observer* tends to support centre left-wing politics. *The Sunday Times*, *Sunday Telegraph* and *Independent on Sunday* are all owned by dailies.

Sunday papers in recent years have put on weight! Many broadsheets are not just papers, they are three or four papers and a handful of magazines. The increased content may be one reason why sales of quality Sundays have remained steady over the past 25 years while the popular papers have lost sales.

Newspaper language

The 'language' of newspapers is not just the words that appear in them. As with other media languages, it includes the pictures that are used, different **font** styles and sizes in text and headings and the way these things are put together in the layout of the page.

No aspect of the way newspapers are put together is an accident. At every stage of production people are making decisions which affect the way the paper looks, reads ... and sells!

The copy

Copy is written by journalists called reporters. Writing for newspapers is very different from the sort of writing done by, say, a novelist. News reporters need to get across the maximum amount of information in the shortest possible time. They also aim to get the 'bare bones' of the story established in the first sentence or two – if you are hooked into the story from the very start you will carry on reading.

Journalists are taught to KISS – Keep It Short and Simple. They used also to be taught to get the 'Five Ws' – Who? What? Where? When? Why? – into the first sentences of their story. Now styles of writing for newspapers have moved on. Trying to pack in all five Ws made for indigestible sentences and this rule is not always followed to the letter – but as a guideline it still offers a helpful starting point.

> ### ACTIVITY 4
>
> 1 Look at the opening two sentences from the main front page story in three different newspapers: two tabloids and one broadsheet. How many of the Five Ws has the reporter managed to get in for each story?
>
> 2 Now do the same for three stories from inside the papers.

The pictures

The first newspapers printed three hundred years ago had very few pictures – and those pictures were drawings because, of course, the camera had not been invented. Nowadays news photographs play a very important part in the whole look of a newspaper, especially the front page.

Look in **7** and **8** at how two newspapers set out their front pages reporting on two of the biggest international news stories of the past 100 years.

Both events were highly significant in the Western world. Almost anyone who was alive at the time remembers exactly what they were doing when they first heard the news of President Kennedy's assassination or the terrorist attack on New York's twin towers. Nearly 40 years separates these two front pages, and the style of newspaper layout changed dramatically between the two events.

> ### ACTIVITY 5
>
> Look carefully at front pages **7** and **8**, paying special attention to the photographs.
>
> 1 Why do you think the **picture editors** chose these particular images? What does each tell us about the story?
>
> 2 What do you think they wanted the reader to feel about each event? What is it about the way the pictures have been presented that helps to influence how the reader feels?

KEY TERMS

Anchor pin down a particular meaning of a drawing or photograph

Angle the particular point of view a newspaper wants its readers to take on a story

Caption words underneath a picture

Copy printed articles that appear in newspapers

Font the different styles of lettering used in printing papers

Picture editor person responsible for choosing the photographs that go into a newspaper

7 Front page of the *Daily Express*, 21 November 1963

8 Front page of *The Times*, 12 September 2001

Captions

People say that 'a picture is worth a thousand words'. Certainly the photograph of New York after the attack on the twin towers in **8** says a great deal about the event. The caption that goes with a photograph is also very important because it can **anchor** a meaning – it tries to push the reader towards one **angle** by providing an interpretation for them. Look at photograph **9**. There could be a number of interpretations made of this image. However, choosing suitable captions could alter the way people read it.

● *South Africa's government has managed to re-house many of its people from tin shacks into solid, brick-built houses:* this caption gives a positive slant on the picture.

● *Unemployment still blights South Africa's townships:* this caption gives a very different, more negative meaning.

9 Street scene in Khayelitsha, South Africa

10

11

Where do newspapers get their photographs? There are three main sources:

- A photographer specifically sent to the scene of the story to cover the story will send back the best possible shots under the circumstances.

- Photos can be set up after the event where there is much more chance to pose the subjects and get a good composition.

- Photos not originally taken as news pictures are used because they are the only available images, for example school photographs of a missing child or images taken from security cameras.

Headlines

Good headlines are crucial, especially on the front page – this headline will draw a purchaser's attention to the paper when it is on the shelf among its competitors. Broadsheet editors will try to draw readers to their stories by using concise headlines which sometimes also give the newspaper's angle on the story, but tabloid headlines are large and catchy.

The Sun has become famous for its controversial headlines. Although these can be amusing, they sometimes cross the line from humour into bad taste. In 1989 the paper printed the headline THE TRUTH above an article about the Hillsborough football disaster in which 95 Liverpool fans were killed. *The Sun*'s 'truth' was that the disaster was caused by drunk Liverpool fans behaving badly. Sales of the paper in Liverpool collapsed, with many newsagents refusing to stock it, and have never recovered.

Techniques	Examples
Abbreviating names	David Beckham is usually 'Becks'.
Parody: taking a well known saying and giving it a slight twist	BRAWL OVER BAR THE SHOUTING
Incorrect or invented spelling	SVENTASTIC for football manager Sven-Goran Eriksson
Alliteration	BILL BOUNCES BACK
Pun: a play on words, often giving a double meaning	BOOTIFUL – winning goal in Cup Final
Rhyming	RIO GIVES HEAVE-HO TO THE MUMBO JUMBO

12 Tricks of the headline-writer's trade

ACTIVITY 8

1   In chart **12** you can see some techniques that headline writers use to draw readers in. Look through a copy of one of the tabloids. Try to find examples of headlines using any of these techniques.

2   Take any story from the same paper and try to make up your own headline using a different technique to the one already used by the paper.

Masthead

Dateline

Earpiece area

Strapline

Splash Head
Full caps

WOB
(white on black)

Underscored

4 colour pic

By-line

Page lead

Support story

Caption

Cross-reference

Thursday November 9 2000

The Mirror

www.mirror.co.uk

Paula's final hours
PAGES 12 & 13

U.S. HUMILIATED IN PRESIDENTIAL SHAMBLES

FORREST CHUMPS

❝This election's like a box of chocolates. You never know what you're gonna get❞

From DAVID LEIGH, Foreign Editor in Texas
AMERICA is without a new president today after its election ended in confusion and farce.

In a night of drama, TV stations declared George W Bush the winner and Al Gore accepted defeat — then backtracked as a recount was called in Florida.

Bush was favourite to win as counting went on but the result may not be known until tonight. President Bill Clinton said: "The American people have spoken. It's just going to take a little while to figure out what they have said."

The drama left the men fighting to be America's 43rd president looking like a pair of Forrest Gumps, the bumbling character from the Tom Hanks hit film.

SEE PAGES 2, 3, 4 AND 5

BROWN GOES GREEN ON FUEL

TAX CUTS: Brown yesterday

GORDON Brown launched a green revolution yesterday in a bid to scupper a new round of fuel protests.

The Chancellor unveiled a £1.75billion package which he said would cut costs by the equivalent of 5p a litre for lorries and 4p for cars.

Despite the pledges, fuel activists

By JAMES HARDY, Political Editor

threatened a new wave of direct action starting with a motorway convoy tomorrow.

In a sparkling Commons performance giving his pre-Budget report,

Mr Brown left the Tories in tatters. Labour MPs cheered as he announced his £5billion giveaway which included a one-off winter fuel payment of £200, a big rise in pensions, £200million for school improvements and a string of measures to boost firms.

Mr Brown also scrapped plans to

raise tax on petrol by 1.5p in next March's Budget. The freeze – revealed exclusively by The Mirror on Monday – comes on top of a penny cut last year.

He trimmed the levy on "green" ultra low sulphur petrol by 2p a

TURN TO PAGE 7

13 The features of newspaper layout

Layout

When all the copy is written and all the photographs have been chosen, the final choices concern how the page is to be laid out. Layout is a key part of the battle to grab the reader's attention and hang on to it.

The **sub-editors** of the paper use computer technology to set out the pages. They work from a page grid that breaks the page into a series of columns. In the past pages were almost always set out in columns, with nothing breaking the grid pattern. Modern page design very often allows both photographs and text to spill outside rigid columns to create dramatic visual impact.

In **13** a front page from *The Mirror* has been marked up with the terms used by sub-editors to describe modern newspaper layout.

Newspapers are constantly researching the ways in which people read pages. They have found, for example, that:

- headlines near photographs are read more than those placed further away
- using colour does not make a story more likely to be read
- people reading a paper look at most of the photographs, artwork and headlines – but much less of the copy.

Above all, a newspaper wants to achieve an individual visual style. This is about individual preferences. What people in Britain regard as good page design may not be what people in other countries like.

TIP

Knowing the terms to describe newspaper layout will help you to know what to look for when writing about them, and increase your marks.

KEY TERM

Sub-editor person responsible for the layout of a newspaper

ACTIVITY 9

Look at the two European front pages in **14** and **15**.

1. Make some notes on the differences you notice between them, using the terms shown in **13**. You could use a chart like the one below.

Le Télégramme	Neue Zürcher Zeitung
Large main photo	Small photo

2. Now note down the differences you can find between each of these front pages and the British front page design in **13**.

Votre jardin. Les tendances du fleurissement estival. Page 49

0.75 €

Le Télégramme

Directeur de la publication : Édouard Coudurier.

CHATEAULIN

N° LECTEURS : 08 20 04 06 29 · e-mail : telegramme@bretagne-online.com

N° 17.977 VENDREDI 11 AVRIL 2003

BRETAGNE

TITRE DE REINE : UN TRÉSOR À PROTÉGER

La Fronde gronde : quatre cercles celtiques du Nord-Finistère ont tenté de s'accaparer l'élection de la Reine du Léon et du Trégor ! Face à cette jacquerie, les tenants de l'ancien régime relèvent les points-levis : du nord au sud, les titres de reine sont devenus des manques déposées.
Dernière page, l'article de Didier Déniel

SÉCURITÉ ROUTIÈRE :
100 € LA BANANE !
Dernière page, le billet de René Perez

PNEUMOPATHIE :
TRANSFERT D'UN BRESTOIS À RENNES
Page 10

FRANCE

CONCORDE :
FIN D'UNE LÉGENDE
Page 8

SPORTS

2007 : LA COUPE DU MONDE EN FRANCE

Battue sur le pré par l'Angleterre dans le Tournoi des six nations, la France a pris sa revanche sur le terrain politique en obtenant, hier, l'organisation la Coupe du monde de rugby 2007. Nantes accueillera certaines rencontres.
En sports

L'IRAK FACE À SON DESTIN

Protectorat américain ? Administration sous le contrôle de l'ONU ?
transition ? Alors que les combats se poursuivent, les Irakiens s'in
Pour l'heure, face à un avenir incertain, les scènes de pillages et de
Une situation anarchique à laquelle il est urgent de mettre fin. Page

---

Freitag, 5. Februar 1999 · Nr. 29

Der Zürcher Zeitung 220. Jahrgang

Neue Zürcher Zeitung

INTERNATIONALE AUSGABE

Heute mit: «Spektrum Deutschlands»

Ausdehnung der Heroinversuche in Holland

Das niederländische Parlament hat am Mittwoch beschlossen, dass ein wissenschaftliches Experiment mit der Vergabe von Heroin unter medizinischer Kontrolle auf 750 Schwerstdrogenabhängige ausgedehnt werden kann. Seit dem Sommer vergangenen Jahres waren zunächst ungesamt 50 Süchtige in Amsterdam und Rotterdam behandelt worden. Nachdem festgestellt worden ist, dass die Fixerstuben keine wesentliche Störung für die Umgebung darstellen, werden sich nun auch die Städte Den Haag, Utrecht und Heerlen an der Grossvergabe der schwereren Droge beteiligen.

HEUTE IN DER NZZ

INTERNATIONAL

Amnesty untersucht Gewalt in Nordirland
Amnesty International will die Menschenrechtsverletzungen in Nordirland untersuchen, die trotz den Friedensverhandlungen andauern.

Die USA zum Eingreifen in Kosovo bereit
Die Vereinigten Staaten sind bereit, sich an der Aufschlagung einer Friedenstruppe für die jugoslawische Provinz Kosovo zu beteiligen, falls ein Friedensabkommen zustande kommt.

Karnevalverstimmung in Rio de Janeiro
In Rio de Janeiro will sich die erste offizielle Karnevalsaune nicht einstellen. Die Krise des Real reisst am Geldbeutel der Cariocas, wie am preislichen Rail des Präsidenten.

WIRTSCHAFT

Die «braunen» Zeit der Deutschen Bank
Die Deutsche Bank hat nach Erkenntnissen ihrer eigenen Historiker während der Nazi-Zeit noch an der Finanzierung von Bauvorhaben im Konzentrations- und Vernichtungslager Auschwitz mitgewirkt.

SCHWEIZ

Krankenversicherungsgesetz unter der Lupe
Eine Analyse von Wirkungen des neuen Krankenversicherungsgesetzes bestätigt die Belastung der Mittelstandes durch die Prämien. Der Risikoausgleich unter den Kassen wird nur begrenzt erreicht.

Neutralität ist nicht Passivität
Es besteht kein Anlass, die schweizerische Neutralität aufzugeben. Aber die Gestaltungspotential könnte und müsste wesentlich besser genutzt werden.

Kontroverse um Paul Grüninger
Gegen Paul Grüninger, der vor dem Zweiten Weltkrieg Juden die Einreise in die Schweiz ermöglicht hatte, ist der Verdacht von Nazi-Sympathien erhoben worden. Dessen Urheber und zwei Kritiker äussern sich dazu.

ZÜRICH

Neuregelung der Spitzenmedizin
Eine im Auftrag der Gesundheitsdirektion erarbeiteter Bedarfs- und Strukturanalyse schlägt die Neuorganisation der spezialisierten und hochspezialisierten Spitzenversorgung vor. Empfohlen wird die Bildung von Leistungsschwerpunkten.

FEUILLETON

Valerio Olgiatis Schulhaus in Paspels
Der von Valerio Olgiati neu errichteten Schulhausbau in Paspels setzt Valerio Olgiati dem Rohti mit einem durch formale Kargheit geprägten Meisterwerk fort.

SPORT

Gründung einer Anti-Doping-Agentur
Als Fazit aus der Weltkonferenz zum Kampf gegen den Dopingmissbrauch in Lausanne ist die Gründung einer Anti-Doping-Agentur beschlossen worden.

VERMISCHTE MELDUNGEN

Kampagne gegen den Aberglauben in China
In China möchten immer mehr Leute ihr Heil im Aberglauben. Wo der Wettbewerbsdruck zu gross wird, muss den sich viele an Wahrsager, um einen Ausweg aus der Abhängmisere zu finden.

BEILAGE

Medien und Informatik
407 Neuntes Musik files Asterodia. Die englische Firma Lenpuq will einen Asterodia austeilen, der sich als Abspielgerät für digitale Musik eignet. Es lassen sich damit bis zu 67 Stunden Musik speichern.

Inhaltsübersicht 2

Grünes Licht für Kosovo-Verhandlungen
Teilnahme von serbischen und albanischen Delegationen

Zu den Friedensverhandlungen über Kosovo werden serbische und albanische Delegationen erscheinen. Die Gespräche werden wohl ohne die Hauptpersonen, Albright und Milosevic, beginnen. Die westlichen Mächte lassen die Entwaldung von Nato-Truppen nicht bein im Auge, Belgrad lehnt dies aber kategorisch ab.

Der jordanische König in kritischem Zustand

Amman, 4. Febr. (Reuter) Der Gesundheitszustand des krebskranken jordanischen Königs Hussein hat sich am Donnerstag nach offiziellen Angaben deutlich verschlechtert. Der jordanische Botschafter in den USA erklärte, die Monarch befinde sich nach dem Versagen eines inneren Organs in kritischem Zustand.

Erneut Verurteilung eines chinesischen Dissidenten
Die jüngste Repressionswelle erfasst auch unautorisierte Arbeiterproteste

Wegen angeblicher Finanzierung subversiver Aktivitäten ist der in Spanien ansässige chinesische Bürgerrechtler Wang Ce in Hangzhou (Provinz Zhejiang) zu einer vierjährigen Haftstrafe verurteilt worden. Die jüngste Repressionswelle gegen Andersdenkende erfasst auch nicht autorisierte Arbeiterproteste.

Demonstration bei Hamburg gegen den Atomausstieg

Net news

Editions of newspapers have been available on the Internet since the mid 1990s. The electronic version of the *Daily Telegraph* was the first to appear in 1994. Now all the major national dailies have web editions.

The Internet edition of a newspaper will include all the content of a printed version: news, sport, horoscopes, crosswords and advertisements.

ACTIVITY 10

1   Compare a version of a national daily with its electronic version. You can access the electronic versions of the ten national dailies via the Heinemann Hotlinks site. What do you think are the strengths and weaknesses of each format? Think about:

  • layout

  • the information available

  • how easy it is to read each version of the newpaper

  • how up-to-date the news is.

2   Now find out if your local paper has a website. Follow the links via Heinemann Hotlinks to a list of all web addresses for electronic newspapers. How does the Internet version compare with the print version?

You probably found that one of the main differences between the printed and electronic versions of papers is the amount of information that an Internet newspaper can carry. If you look at the home page of any of the Internet papers you will find all sorts of things it simply would not be possible for a printed paper to include. For example, the *Mirror* site allows you to look back through front pages from the previous two years and the Film section carries many more reviews than it would be possible to put in a daily print edition. The ability to link through to already existing web pages allows an electronic newspaper to give readers access to a host of additional information.

Another difference is that you can read the printed version of the newspaper anywhere, whereas to read the electronic version you have to use your computer. As technology advances, however, and electronic newspapers can be accessed on mobile phones and palmtop computers, this difference may diminish.

And finally, Internet papers can be updated throughout the day with 'breaking news'. This brings newspapers closer to the broadcast media in their ability to provide the latest news.

 ## Representing the world

'A newspaper ought to be the register of the times and faithful recorder of every species of intelligence.' This famous quote was written over two hundred years ago by John Walter, the first editor of *The Times*. The word 'intelligence' means what is now called 'news'. For Walter, there did not appear to be a problem about 'faithfully recording' events of the day. As newspaper journalism has developed over time it has become obvious that it is never easy to avoid being biased or inaccurate.

Fact?

John Walter seemed to think that newspapers should mainly report facts. The three front pages shown in images **16** to **18** appeared on the day after the Paddington rail disaster in 1999. They show that sometimes the facts can be a bit different, depending on which paper you are reading them in.

16 Front page of the *Daily Express*, 6 October 1999

18 Front page of *The Mirror*, 6 October 1999

17 Front page of the *Daily Mail*, 6 October 1999

At least *The Daily Express* used a question mark in its headline. Readers are invited to think about the awful possibility that a huge number of people were killed, but while 'the grim hunt goes on' there will remain a doubt about numbers. *The Mirror* and the *Daily Mail* both state – quite clearly and boldly – an actual number of dead.

ACTIVITY 11

Discuss in pairs *why* you think each newspaper chose the front page it did.

1 Why did *The Daily Express* use such a high number? Why might it have felt the need to show there was some doubt about the number by posing a question rather than stating a fact?

2 Why did the other two papers present the number of dead as a fact?

Opinion

It is often not the facts that are given but the opinions of the reporters, editors or their sources that introduce an angle. Sometimes the papers make it obvious that they are expressing an opinion. **Leader articles** on the Editorial page set out what the paper's editor or owner thinks should be done about a particular issue. These usually discuss serious topics – whether Britain should join the Euro or whether it should go to war, for example.

But often the way news events are reported builds a certain point of view into the story. In this case the angle is governed by the choices editorial staff make – the paper chooses the viewpoint it wants to put across to its readers.

News is often reported in terms of *heroes* and *villains*. Sometimes it is easy. Saddam Hussein was rarely represented as anything other than an out-and-out villain who had killed thousands of his own people and spent Iraq's oil wealth on himself. However, sports personalities and teams often swing quickly from being heroes to villains and back again within a matter of days. News reports always try to tell a story.

ACTIVITY 12

Using a copy of any national daily newspaper, find three stories that present the reader with clear heroes and villains.

1 Which words from the articles make you think that one person is the 'goody' and the other is the 'baddy'?

2 Are any pictures used to support the view you are given of the characters in the piece?

News sources

It is important to know about **news sources** because how newspapers represent the news of the day is affected by the sources from which that news comes.

Over 60 per cent of all newspaper stories come from **press releases** or press conferences. A busy local paper will often print a well written press release, following the Five Ws and KISS rules, almost as it stands. If you want your school play to be given a good press, you need a good press release, describing your 'gripping' performance of a 'much loved classic' play. In Media Studies terms, you will have achieved a **positive representation** of the production.

ACTIVITY 13

Write a press release for an event in your area. This could be a sports event, a live music concert, a non-uniform day – anything you think your local paper ought to cover. Remember the Five Ws and KISS!

Generally speaking, local newspapers get their news from:

- Agendas for meetings, e.g. the County Council, the local Health Authority Trust, the Steam Railway Preservation Society
- Press releases sent by email and post from various organisations
- Police or Fire and Rescue services
- News Agencies such as the Press Association and Reuters
- Members of the public telling the paper of incidents or events
- Contacts: people the paper's journalists call regularly to see if they have a story; occasionally these people will call the paper to tip them off about an event.

KEY TERM

Source find information to use when writing news stories

This list might lead you to think that journalists could go to many different places to **source** their news. However, research has shown that they use a remarkably limited range. If the sources are limited then so will be the view of the world the papers give us.

Journalists put sources into the following three categories:

Primary sources: the courts, police, fire service, Members of Parliament, organisations representing business and industry, trade unions, football clubs

Secondary sources: schools, churches, charities, representatives of pressure groups such as Friends of the Earth

Alternative sources: representatives of religions other than Christianity, ethnic minority groups, feminist, lesbian and gay groups, anti-war groups such as CND, representatives of political parties other than the main three.

Critics say that the routines used by journalists for sourcing news mean that their stories reflect the distribution of power in the country. People from the leading groups and institutions have easier access to the press and so their views are heard more often. Representatives from 'alternative' groups get little or no press coverage and this reinforces their powerlessness in society.

ACTIVITY 14

1 Examine any national or local newspaper. Choose three news stories. Try to work out which news sources might have provided each story. Use this list to help you:
   - A press conference given by an organisation
   - A press release from an organisation
   - Parliament
   - The emergency services
   - Member of the public directly contacting the paper
   - A detailed investigation by one of the paper's reporters.

2 Choose one of the three stories that seems to have a clear angle on the events it describes. What would the alternative viewpoint be on this story? Where might the journalist have had to go to get an alternative angle?

News values

Most journalists will tell you that selecting the right stories for the day is a matter of experience and instinct. But in a famous study in 1973 Galtang and Ruge found that these factors help a story to get into the news:

- *Timescale:* a murder is committed and discovered quickly, so it fits the timescale on which newspapers work. An increase in gun crime, which happens over a long period, will only get reported when there are a series of gun-related crimes.

- *The size of an event:* A rail crash killing 25 people is big news; a train derailment with no injuries is not.

- *How clear the event is:* News need not be simple, but a very complicated story will probably get left out.

- *Predictability:* If the press expects something to happen then it will. A big anti-capitalist demonstration planned for central London will get reported, even if it passes off peacefully, because the press expect violence and send journalists to cover it.

- *Continuity:* A running story, like a war, will continue to be covered.

- *Reference to elite people or nations:* News about the USA or their president is more likely to get covered than similar news from Costa Rica.

News coverage is often **ethnocentric**. How do newspapers, and other media, report on less developed countries? These nations appear in the news when there are famines, natural disasters, violent revolutions or political corruption. Readers are invited to be thankful that they live in a stable country, where everyone has the basics of life and is fairly and honestly governed. But can it *really* be true that nothing good ever happens in the developing world?

Newspapers are said to give a 'window on the world', but in reality they give the view from a window facing in only one direction. Behind the other three walls there are all sorts of things going on, but they do not get reported.

ACTIVITY 15

1 Conduct your own survey into the news values of one tabloid daily paper for a week. Without reading them in full, complete a tally chart like the one below.

   - Count the total number of news stories each day.
   - Count the number of stories about Africa each day, adding that as a second column to your chart.
   - Of the stories which you found about Africa, make a note of how many were giving good news about the country and how many were reporting problems.

Day	News stories	Stories about Africa	Good news	Bad news
Monday	17	3	1	2

2 At the end of the week, choose the three 'biggest' news stories. Try to work out how many of the points on Galtang and Ruge's list apply to each story.

KEY TERM

Ethnocentric biased towards events in the country in which the paper is produced

Newspaper audiences

Why do newspapers need to know about their audiences?
The running costs of a newspaper have to be covered by:

- money from the sale of newspapers, which depends on the **circulation figure**

- money provided by advertisers taking space in the paper. The bigger the **readership**, the more they can charge people to advertise.

Just like any other media industry, it is very important for newspapers to know how large their readership is and how that readership breaks down in terms of gender and social class.

Advertising has an obvious effect on the way a paper looks. **Display adverts** create visual impact. In fact, when sub-editors lay up a page they put in the advertisements first.

- Some papers try to avoid placing adverts on certain pages, such as the front page.

- Advertisers sometimes pay more to ensure their product is the only one advertised on a page.

- Advertisers try to avoid the sports pages, so the remaining pages may have a high proportion of advertising content.

- It is the adverts, not the news, which determine how many pages an issue has: more adverts, a bigger paper!

How do newspapers find out about their readers?
Both advertisers and newspapers classify their readership into **socio-economic groups**; readers in the A, B and C1 categories will have more money to spend on things they see advertised.

Within those categories, newspapers use information from the National Readership Survey about different genders, particular interest groups – like car drivers or home owners – and age groups. You can see information from the NRS website in **19**. Just to be sure the newspapers are telling them the truth, advertisers can go to the Audit Bureau of Circulation, which checks that circulation figures are correct.

Daily Newspapers Monday to Saturday Average readership	Adults													
	Total adults		ABC1		C2DE		15–44		45+		Men		Women	
	000s	%	000s	%	000s	%	000s	%	000s	%	000s	%	000s	%
The Sun	9229	19.6	3267	12.9	5962	27.3	5652	23.6	3577	15.5	5220	22.8	4009	16.5
Daily Mail	5979	12.7	3955	15.7	2024	9.3	2093	8.7	3886	16.8	3022	13.2	2957	12.2
Daily Mirror	5146	10.9	1990	7.9	3155	14.4	2318	9.7	2828	12.2	2727	11.9	2419	10.0
Daily Telegraph	2306	4.9	1967	7.8	339	1.6	702	2.9	1604	6.9	1268	5.5	1038	4.3
Daily Express	2181	4.6	1307	5.2	874	4.0	767	3.2	1414	6.1	1161	5.1	1020	4.2
Daily Star	1894	4.0	649	2.6	1245	5.7	1347	5.6	547	2.4	1362	6.0	533	2.2
The Times	1865	4.0	1635	6.5	230	1.1	894	3.7	971	4.2	1115	4.9	750	3.1
Metro	1498	3.2	973	3.9	525	2.4	1139	4.7	359	1.6	874	3.8	624	2.6
The Guardian	1332	2.8	1144	4.5	189	0.9	771	3.2	562	2.4	776	3.4	557	2.3
The Independent	584	1.2	497	2.0	87	0.4	308	1.3	276	1.2	370	1.6	214	0.9

19 Information from the National Readership Survey, June 2002–June 2003

ACTIVITY 16

1 Which of the papers listed has the largest daily readership? What figure does the table give for this paper?

2 If you were an advertiser with a product you wanted to sell to socio-economic groups ABC1, which paper would you approach first?

3 In which papers, apart from *The Sun*, would you advertise:

- trainers
- *Guide to Eating Out in London*
- holidays for the over-50s?

UNIT SUMMARY

Key area	What you have learned
Media language	• The codes and conventions which are used by newspapers when writing about the news.
Audiences	• That different newspapers target different readerships. • Readers use newspapers in different ways.
Institutions and organisations	• That the political viewpoint of a newspaper owner or the sources from which news comes can affect the way information is presented to readers.
Representation	• That news values affect what gets into the news and how much coverage individual stories receive. • That the way individuals, groups or ideas are portrayed will depend on the viewpoint of the newspaper and its journalists.

4 Magazines

In this unit you will find out:

- how to identify the features of the content and presentation of magazines
- how a magazine targets and is used by its audience
- how institutions and organisations influence magazines both through ownership and paying for advertising
- how stars and celebrities are represented in magazines.

TALKING POINT

- Why do you choose the magazines you read?
- Do you read magazines while you are doing something else, such as talking with friends?
- Where do you read them?
- Do you always read the same magazines or do you choose a different one each time?

Categorising magazines

Go into any newsagent, garage or supermarket. The choice of magazines to buy in the twenty-first century is staggering. Looking at the way they are displayed will help you to understand what types of magazines there are.

1 Magazines displayed in a store

ACTIVITY 1

Prepare yourself for studying magazines by going into your local newsagent or looking at **1**. Stand back and look at the rows of magazines on the shelves.

- What are your first impressions of the display?
- How have the magazines been arranged?
- Do any colours stand out strongly? Which ones?
- What features on the covers tell you what time of year it is?
- Do any faces appear on more than one magazine? Whose?
- Which subjects or themes are covered by more than one magazine?

TIP

Start a topic notebook to jot down your thoughts and ideas.

One obvious way to start **categorising** magazines is to split them up into general interest and specialist groups. General interest magazines, such as *Woman's Weekly*, have a broad range of subject matter, covering lots of topics and issues. Specialist magazines, such as *Formula 1*, are tailored to a particular area of interest. Think about the magazines you read – which category do they go in?

ACTIVITY 2

Work in a pair or small group. Decide whether each of these magazine titles is in the general interest or the specialist category. The first two have been done for you.

General interest magazines	Specialist magazines
OK	Empire

- OK
- Empire
- Go Girl!
- New Woman
- Rugby World
- PC Format
- Heat

- Radio Times
- Men's Health
- Dogs Today
- Cosmopolitan
- Digital Photography
- Family Circle
- Bob the Builder

- Hair
- Good Housekeeping
- Popgirl
- Mizz
- Glamour
- My First Magazine
- Woman's Own

There are many other ways of categorising magazines, for example in terms of the companies that publish them. Magazine publishers are often part of large, sometimes huge, international media conglomerates that also own newspapers, and radio and television stations.

KEY TERM

Categorise order or group similar texts, e.g. magazines, according to the features they have in common

- IPC has nearly 100 UK brands, including *NME*, and sells a magazine every 11 seconds throughout the year.

- EMAP, publisher of *Smash Hits!*, has 150 top-selling consumer magazines in the UK, France and around the world, as well as radio, TV and music brands.

- BBC Worldwide is the third largest consumer magazine publisher in the UK. Titles include *BBC History Magazine* and *Radio Times*.

- National Magazine Company is a subsidiary of the vast Hearst Corporation in America. It publishes seventeen high-circulation consumer magazines in the UK, including *Cosmopolitan* and *Esquire*.

- Future is a smaller company based in Bath specialising in film, computing and sports magazines, including fanzines such as *United*.

ACTIVITY 3

1   Research the publishers and circulations of the magazines in Activity 2. Follow the link on Heinemann Hotlinks. Display your results in a table.

Magazine	Publisher	Circulation
OK		

2   Look at your tables from this activity and Activity 2. Which types of magazines have the highest and lowest circulations?

Analysing magazine covers

Magazine publishing is a hugely profitable and growing media industry. It is also very competitive. Your research in Activity 1 showed you some techniques used by magazines to address their audiences by capturing their interest on the shelf. Now you are going to look closely at a magazine cover and analyse its features. This is an excellent way to find out what messages a magazine is conveying to its audience.

To be successful a magazine must establish a close, personal and almost friendly relationship with its readers. Magazines are all about **mode of address**. This is often through the person featured in the text. On the cover in **2** the person is looking straight out at the reader; this is known as a *direct mode of address*. When the person is looking away, and therefore inviting the reader to look on, but to be less involved, the text is using an *indirect mode of address*. This gives clues about the type of magazine it is and the relationship it wants to have with its audience.

Now look at the annotations on **2**. You already know what *mode of address* means. Try to make sure that you understand the other terms in **bold** that are used in the annotations. It is important to use the correct terms when you analyse any media text. Other key terms that you might use when you analyse a magazine cover are:

- **seasonal theme**: when the colours and contents of a magazine relate to the time of year, e.g. red hearts and features on romance for St Valentine's Day

- **mise-en-scene**: the way in which every element of the text is arranged to create a meaning

- **anchorage text**: writing that fixes the meaning of an image, e.g. a caption

- **blurb**: factual information, often in small print.

The **price** is placed in an eye-catching 'star' to attract the eye and act as a persuasive technique.

The **slogan** tries to convince the reader that this magazine is better than its rivals.

The **central image** of Kym Marshall relies on the audience knowing that she was in the band Hearsay and married Jack Ryder from *EastEnders*. Kym is represented in a fashionable dress that shows off her figure – the **anchorage text** suggests that she has lost weight – and she uses **direct mode of address**, smiling into the eyes of the reader to share her happiness with them.

The **title** of the magazine connotes an up-to-the-minute feel, suggesting that readers will be reading the most recent events in the lives of the celebrities featured.

The word 'exclusive' is a **buzz word** suggesting that this magazine is the only one to cover this story.

The arrow is a **graphic feature** to add interest to the question being posed.

Puffs at the bottom of the page suggest that the magazine will give fashion and beauty tips – assuming that the reader is concerned with their appearance.

The three **images** are linked by theme – they all feature stars and their babies – and by the story title which acts as **anchorage text**. The story relies on the audience knowing who the stars are and that they are now parents. It also assumes that readers want to know about the private lives of stars.

2 Analysing a magazine cover

Now have a go at analysing the magazine front cover in **3** yourself. *Hotdog* is a specialist film magazine aimed at 15–35-year-old males with an interest in film. Try to identify how the cover has been made to appeal to its audience.

- Remember to use the correct terms whenever you can.

- Look back at how the cover in **2** was analysed if you need help.

3 *Hotdog*'s readers are mainly male filmgoers aged 15 to 35 years

Who reads magazines?

Considering the ways in which audiences read or watch different media texts is a very important part of media studies. The best way to start is with YOU, since so many texts are aimed at people like you. You are part of the powerful 14–18-year-old audience, and media producers are very interested to know what you like and what you want.

Can you think why your age group is so powerful? The main reason is that, even though you don't usually earn large sums of money, what you do earn is virtually all **disposable income** – there is only you to spend it on. After all, most young people do not have to pay for food or housing, so media producers want you to spend your money on their products. Producers also want readers with spending power to attract advertisers who subsidise the cost of production. The money advertisers pay for space in print-based texts is used to reduce the selling price. Without **subsidisation**, print-based media texts would cost over twice as much.

When and how do people consume media texts?

Audiences consume, that is, watch, read or listen to, media products in a whole range of situations and places, sometimes while doing other things, sometimes with focused attention. This is sometimes known as *pattern of consumption*. How is the girl in **4** consuming the text?.

4 People consume media products in different ways

ACTIVITY 5

You are going to analyse the media you consume.

1   Keep a diary for one week of all the TV and radio programmes, films, CDs, magazines and so on that you consume. This will be your **media consumption** diary.

    • Note how long you spend on each text.

    • Write down whether you were a **primary consumer** or a **secondary consumer**.

    A typical diary might start like this:

Friday 5th March, 2004
1 Listened to the radio while getting dressed. 45 minutes. Secondary
2 Watched C4 while having breakfast. 45 minutes. Secondary
3 Listened to Counting Crows CD on way to school. 20 minutes. Primary

2   Add up your consumption of each type of media for the week. Choose a way to show your results, e.g. a bar graph, table or pie chart.

3   Write a few paragraphs about your media consumption during the week. You may wish to use these headings: *Film, TV, Radio, Magazines and newspapers, Own music, the Internet.*

    • Why did you choose the texts you consumed?

    • Are there any media texts you deliberately chose not to consume? Why?

KEY TERMS

Media consumption
the media texts you watch, listen to or read

Primary consumer
someone absolutely focused on watching, listening to or reading a media text

Secondary consumer
someone watching, listening to or reading a media text while doing something else, such as talking or homework

Why do people consume media texts?

Blumler and Katz suggested in the 1970s that media audiences make *active* choices about what to consume in order to meet certain needs. Their Uses and Gratifications Theory tries to show the different reasons that audiences have for consuming certain media texts.

The Uses and Gratifications Theory

Media consumers choose texts that fulfil one or more of these needs:

- the need to be INFORMED and EDUCATED about the world in which they live

- the need to IDENTIFY personally with characters and situations in order to learn more about themselves

- the need to be ENTERTAINED by a range and variety of well constructed texts

- the need to use the media as a talking point for SOCIAL INTERACTION

- the need to ESCAPE from their 'daily grind' into other worlds and situations.

ACTIVITY 6

Try applying the Uses and Gratifications theory to the media you enjoy.

1   Choose any television programme you enjoy. Explain how the Uses and Gratifications theory can be used to show why you love it. An example has been given to help you.

> I enjoy watching 'Big Brother' because I like to choose which characters are most like me and who act like I would in the house (IDENTIFY). It is really good fun to watch the housemates make such fools of themselves (ENTERTAINED). My friends enjoy 'Big Brother' too, and sometimes we watch together on eviction night to see who is voted out (SOCIAL INTERACTION). I would never go on 'Big Brother' myself, but it takes my mind off my work (ESCAPE)!

2   Now apply the Uses and Gratifications Theory to a magazine you read regularly.

Another helpful way to talk about an audience is to say whether it is an **active audience** or a **passive audience**. Active audiences may, for example, vote in a magazine poll, choose a different magazine each week, change their loyalty to a magazine as they get older and challenge the assumptions underlying the quiz page. Passive consumers, on the other hand, remain loyal to one magazine for longer, believe what they read without question and may even cheat in the quizzes to have the 'perfect' profile.

Values and lifestyle

Values and lifestyle can also be called **ideology**. At first glance this may seem like a difficult concept, but ideology is simply a term for the way people think about themselves, about others and about the world they live in. The only difficult thing about ideology is that it is so instinctive and unspoken that it is rather invisible. People tend not to know what their values and beliefs are unless they are challenged in some way.

KEY TERMS

Active audience an audience that has a two-way relationship with a media text and can resist the message that it is intended to convey

Ideology a system of values, beliefs or ideas that are common to a specific group of people

Passive audience an audience that consumes a media text by accepting its intended messages without question

Target audiences groups of people, defined by factors such as age, gender, ethnicity and lifestyle, that media texts are aimed at

You may find a surprising level of agreement amongst your ideal choices for these roles. Since you have similar values or ideologies, you will have similar ideas of who best meets the requirements for each role. For example, the leader may well be the most outspoken, popular member of the group, while the emotional support person is likely to be a mature, cheerful person who happily speaks to everyone, and not just their friendship group. The class will have agreed on this because you all understand that, in order to take any of those roles, people need to have demonstrated certain values and standards of behaviour.

Ideological behaviour

Ideologies can be seen on many different levels. Countries have national ideologies: if you go on holiday abroad, you will notice patterns of behaviour that would be unusual in the UK. In Spain, for example, the shops close for several hours in the middle of the day. Can you think of anything that visitors to the UK would notice about our patterns of behaviour? People often say that the British love queuing, for example.

Schools have ideologies, too. What about your school? Are there any systems of behaviour that your school values which students from other schools may find odd? Perhaps you have an unusual reward system for good behaviour.

Now think about your *family ideology* – can you think of any customs that you value and share? Perhaps you celebrate festivals differently from your friends, such as waiting until after Christmas dinner to open your presents.

Understanding ideology is very helpful when it comes to analysing target audiences and the kinds of things they like, dislike and wish for.

Describing audiences

You will need to describe and pinpoint **target audiences** throughout your media course and final exam, so it is worth considering a few ways of defining the audiences for magazines.

Gender

Some texts have an obvious gender bias. *Action Man* and *Girl Talk* are examples of magazines with a clear male/female bias. Sometimes you can identify if gender is a relevant issue by considering themes or values at the heart of a text. Look again at the front cover of *Now* magazine on page 85 – a focus on appearance and image is often associated with female audiences. Some people think that magazines can be harmful by reinforcing female **stereotypes** – for example, girls and women can make themselves ill trying to look like the models in the pictures. What do you think?

Age

Try to avoid making sweeping statements about the age of a target audience, such as: 'This text is aimed at teenagers'. You might find the following breakdown helpful:

Under 5   6–8   9–12   13–15   16–18   19–25   26–40   41–60   Over 60

ACTIVITY 8

Imagine you are a media producer considering at which audience to aim your latest product. What do you know about people of different ages?

List and discuss the probable lifestyle, likes and dislikes of people in these age groups: 6–8; 16–18; 25–40; over 60.

Ask yourself about their hobbies, their favourite night out, the TV programmes they watch, etc. How might a media producer use this information?

People over 60 are likely to: have low disposable income; have similar, non-active lifestyles; not enjoy violence; enjoy films and programmes from the past.

When target audiences are described in this way, the various categories are being stereotyped. The description of people over 60 in Activity 8 may be true for many people, but it is important to remember that some over-60s still earn high salaries, run marathons, enjoy thrillers and go to pop concerts!

Ethnicity

Although ethnicity is not always relevant, the racial or religious background of an audience may be a factor affecting what a text contains. For example, *Asiana Wedding* is a magazine that targets Asian women.

5 Ethnicity is a major factor in the audience targeting of *Asiana Wedding*

ACTIVITY 9

Find out what magazines are most popular with people in your school. Try to ask students who represent a mix of ages, genders and ethnic backgrounds. What links can you see between these factors and the magazines people enjoy? Present your findings in the form of a chart, graph or table and discuss in class.

Lifestyle

Being able to discuss the possible lifestyle and habits of an audience is important. Try to consider the **values and aspirations** (ideology) of the audience of a text you are analysing. Media producers research their audiences well, to find out what kinds of things are important to them, so that the messages in their texts will appeal to them and make them respond positively to them. Ask yourself how the text highlights (and perhaps reinforces) those values.

Look again at the front cover of *Now* magazine on page 85.

● It suggests that the audience might be anxious about their appearance – note the '8 pages of holiday fashion' and Kym's 'diet secrets'.

● The audience are obviously very interested in stories about stars and celebrities, and probably use pictures of them to provide role models of beauty, fame and success.

● The magazine assumes that readers will want to know as much about the personal lives of celebrities as possible, in this case featuring stars and their babies.

6 *Mizz* magazine, November 2003

© MIZZ/IPC Syndication

ACTIVITY 10

Look closely at the front cover of *Mizz* in **6**. Write bullet points to suggest:

• the likely audience of the magazine

• the kinds of features that might be appealing to this audience.

ACTIVITY 11 EXTENSION

In Activity 2 you categorised magazines into General interest and Specialist groups. Now that you understand how magazine targeting works, categorise these magazines into more specific audience categories:

- *Sugar* • *Radio Times* • *Rugby World* • *Good Housekeeping* • *Empire*

KEY TERMS

Celebrity someone who is popular in one country for appearing in one media field, such as soap opera

Representation how the media shape images of people to present them to the audience

Star a performer who is famous internationally

Stars and celebrities

Magazine producers often feature a **star** or **celebrity** on a front cover in order to increase sales, and therefore profit. Which of these famous people would you classify as stars, and which as celebrities?

- Madonna
- Cat Deely
- Dale Winton
- Catherine Zeta Jones
- Emma Bunton
- Sean Connery
- Matt Damon
- Ant and Dec

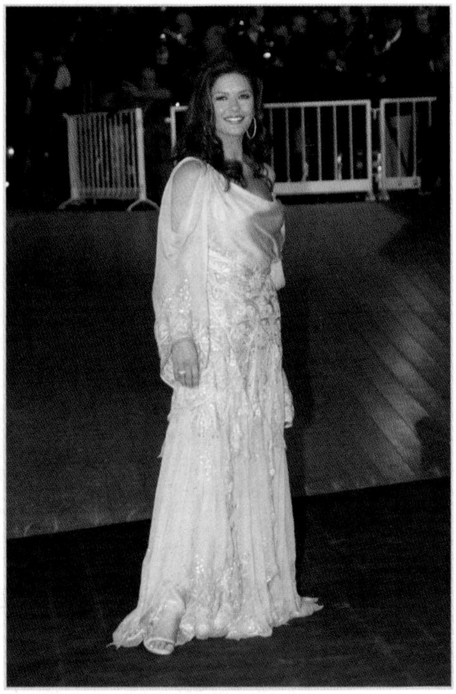

7 Catherine Zeta Jones – celebrity or star?

As a nation, people in the United Kingdom are fascinated by the lives of the famous, but how much is this enthusiasm caused by the wide coverage of celebrities in the UK media? To help answer this question, look at the advertising triangle in **8**.

- Producers make texts that audiences consume and respond to.
- These responses to texts are taken into account by producers when they make more texts.
- Popular formats are repeated, so that audiences are given the sorts of texts they 'ask for'.

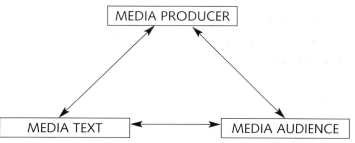

```
                    ┌─────────────────┐
                    │ MEDIA PRODUCER  │
                    └─────────────────┘
                      ↗             ↖
                    ↙                 ↘
  ┌─────────────────┐               ┌─────────────────┐
  │   MEDIA TEXT    │ ←───────────→ │  MEDIA AUDIENCE  │
  └─────────────────┘               └─────────────────┘
```

8 Advertising triangle

Take a few moments to discuss this triangle and the complex relationship between the maker of the magazine, the magazine itself and its target audience. Who has the most power in this process – the producers who make texts, the texts themselves or the audiences who consume and respond to them?

The media are often criticised for constantly representing stars and celebrities, and possibly even intruding into their private lives. However, famous people need the media to maintain their 'stardom', and we, the audience, are greedy for more information about them. Who can you name who has become famous very quickly because of constant media attention? Now think of someone who has received negative media attention.

ACTIVITY 12

Talk with a partner about stars and celebrities and their coverage in the media. Try to decide how far you agree with this statement:

Magazines feature too many stories about stars and celebrities.

How stars are represented

The **representation** of stars and celebrities is worth considering in any media form you are studying. Much has been written about film and television stars, and there are many theories about how and why they achieve fame. Consider this statement: *Stars are people who have become famous in one specialist area of activity who then also achieve attention in other areas.*

9 What are the Beckhams most famous for now? Think about each member of the family in turn

Another way of looking at stars is to say that they are *'complex representations of real people'*. In other words, they are not completely real, but they are based on someone who *is* real. They are people who have been given some kind of image treatment that will affect how audiences see and respond to them. Even though you may feel you know a lot about David Beckham, could you say that you actually know him?

10 Images of Madonna from 2001 and 2003

ACTIVITY 13

Stars are people who have become famous in one specialist area of activity and then also attract attention in other areas.

1   Discuss this quotation with a partner, then feed back and discuss it as a class. Is this quote helpful when considering star/celebrity coverage in magazines? You may find it useful to have a range of magazines to look at.

2   Analyse the representation of one of your favourite stars or celebrities in at least two different magazines. Make a list of similarities and differences. How can the same person be shown differently?

Mise-en-scene

The creation of every image, whether still or moving, involves planning and setting up. The careful arrangement of every element in an image to create a particular message or meaning is called the *mise-en-scene*. The phrase is taken from French and literally means *'put in scene or shot'*.

ACTIVITY 14

1   The best way to understand how mise-en-scene works is to try it out yourself. Imagine you are the producer of a magazine called *School Leaver*. You want the magazine to communicate to its teenage readers that it is cool to be studious and to care about the future, as well as to be popular and trendy. You want to take a picture of a 16-year-old for the front cover. How would you create the mise-en-scene?

    • Choose a suitable setting, e.g. a classroom with good displays. Place a desk and chair in the shot.
    • Choose a subject from your class who you think has the right image for the shot.
    • Wearing school uniform, how will you make sure the subject looks the part?
    • Ask the subject to sit at a desk. How will they position their legs?
    • Which items of stationery, books, etc. will be on the desk? Why?
    • What kind of bag will the subject have?
    • Just before you take the shot, how will you ask the subject to pose?

11 This mise-en-scene makes the subjects look studious

2   When you have taken the photo, try something else. This time you are the producer of *Bliss* magazine for teenage girls aged 11–14. A photo story needs a shot of a two-timing, school-hating, sports-mad teenager who is bored in their lesson and desperate for the bell to go. Using only what you already have from the first mise-en-scene, change the arrangement of the elements to create a different meaning.

    • What changes might you make to the subject's uniform and general 'look'?
    • What might happen to the books and pens?
    • What pose will you ask for this time?

12 The same elements are used here to create a different effect!

ACTIVITY 15

You are going to create a profile for yourself as a star. You can see an example in **13**. Then you are going to take a photograph of yourself as a star to go in a magazine of your choice.

1 Choose an area of specialism, for example a TV celebrity who presents children's programmes.

2 List five bullet points connected to your representation. You could include: *a zany sense of humour, a love of animals which is built into your shows, a famous mother.*

3 Now create a 'look' for yourself that matches your profile. Think carefully about the mise-en-scene of the magazine page, so that the background is as appropriate as your costume and make-up. Set the shot up and ask someone to take the photograph. Make sure that your facial expression creates an impression of your star personality.

TIP

This photograph could be used as part of a piece of coursework.

This weeks star profile...
Alicia Hepworth

Last time we spoke to you you were promoting your first album, now after an outstanding second album, a world tour and a number of festival appearances I'm sure you have a lot more to say for yourself.

So how was the tour?
Some moments were by far some of the best in my life, being live on stage in front of a room full or often an arena full of an audience who are radiating enjoyment and pure love for live and loud music makes me feel so good that often I wish I could jump of the stage and join the party. But there are some moments when you just wish you could be back at home, but the good moments outweigh the bad ones by far.

Your second album seems a lot heavier than your first, is this the direction that you are going to continue moving in?
Before I even actually made my first album the music I played was more like what I have done with my second album, much heavier, its just how I prefer to play. I look back at my first album now and realise that it wasn't me, I way I play now is how I love to play. So yes I guess I will be continuing in that direction but then again you never know what the future has to bring, for all I know in ten years from now I could be the eighth member of Sclub 7.

If they propositioned you would you accept?
Ummmm... (pause) no. Sorry guys not really my scene. Who would you say have influenced you most musically?
I grew up listening to artists such as Hendrix, the Beatles, the Jam, the Who, Jefferson Airplane, David Bowe, Led Zeppelin etc. My general love for rock music and all of these bands

Inspired me to do something myself. As a girl of ten I was playing Hendrix on my first guitar, since then I have never stopped.

I noticed you named mainly artists of the 60's and 70's there. Was this due to parental influence?
To a certain extent yes but I was mainly influenced by my uncle. He would lend me three LP's every week and then he would help me to learn to play the songs on them. This gave me a wide knowledge of music. As a young girl in the early nineties you may have expected me to be listening to bands such as Take That and New Kids on the Block, but I wasn't interested, I guess you could say that my musical tastes were stuck in an era that I was never alive to see.

What are you hoping to achieve form your music career in the future?
Well at the moment I am pretty happy doing what I

am doing at the moment but I would like to travel more at some point. Being in a band would be cool. That's something ive also wanted to do. Being a solo rock artist is good but I have always thought that you can something more out of being in a band. So that is some that I will seriously consider doing in the future.

Finally, apart from the music aspect of your life what would you say has been your best experience in life?
Surfing. I am obsessed. I love everything about it. So maybe it would have to be the best wave I have ever caught.

"You could say that my musical tastes were stuck in an era that I was never alive to see."

13 This star profile was created by a student

Analysing contents pages

14 The contents page from *Dare* magazine, February 2004

You have already seen that you can find out a lot about what a magazine has to offer by looking at its cover. The next step is to look at the contents page. This will give you an overview of what is in the magazine you are studying. You can also see how it has been laid out to catch the reader's attention. Look for:

● the main areas of interest that the magazine covers

● the kinds of features in each area

● how the reader's attention is drawn to special features

● how images and words are combined.

Although every magazine is different, each genre of magazine has typical features. As an example, look at the typical features of a magazine aimed at teenage girls.

● *Contents* – tells the reader how to find their way around the magazine. What first impressions do you get about what this magazine considers to be important?

- *Articles on the opposite sex* – 'how to …' or 'how to improve …'. Although these magazines are bought by girls, boys read them too! Teens of both sexes read about the sexual experiences of others to prepare themselves for their own experiences.

- *The 'true story'* – an immediate hook into the reader's own life as she tries to make links between the story and her real-life experiences.

- *The Quiz* – a fictional but realistic scenario aims to test readers' potential responses in the real world. Quizzes often promote an 'average' response as the best one. If the teenage girl scores the right number of points, she knows she will not stand out as being too different from her peers. This can directly influence the ways that teenage girls see themselves. They are encouraged to conform to certain stereotypes of looks and behaviour, and discouraged from breaking 'out of the mould'.

- *Features about celebrities* – stories about pop, film and TV stars help readers to feel they have a relationship with the 'great' and famous. Nearly everyone is interested in the private lives of public figures.

- *Problem pages* – these give a genuine point of contact. Reading about familiar situations or fears is reassuring and removes feelings of abnormality and separation. Look back at the Uses and Gratifications Theory on page 88 – what needs do problem pages satisfy?

- *Advertising and articles on fashion and beauty* – stereotypical representations of beautiful 'perfect' peers reinforce image and identity and give teenagers a range of products which they can be sure will be acceptable to others. Some advertisements look like feature articles and may cover several pages – these are called *advertorials*.

ACTIVITY 16 EXTENSION

Why are some magazines blamed for having a bad influence on teenagers? Try to refer to two or three examples in your explanation.

UNIT SUMMARY

Key area	What you have learned
Media language	• Terminology for analysing magazine covers. • Techniques for contents analysis.
Audiences	• Different ways that audiences can be identified and targeted. • Why audiences read magazines. • How audiences are affected by the magazines they read. • The difference between primary and secondary consumption.
Institutions and organisations	• How magazines are categorised. • Who owns and produces magazines.
Representation	• How magazines create and represent stars and celebrities. • How mode of address is used in magazines.

5 Comics, cartoons and animation

In this unit you will find out:

- how to recognise the codes and conventions that cartoons and animations use to convey meaning
- how comics and cartoons are used by their audience to satisfy certain needs
- how superhero characters are owned, developed and marketed
- how character types such as heroes and villains are represented in cartoons.

TALKING POINT

- Which comics and animated characters did you like best before you were ten? Share your ideas.
- People often get very excited and animated when they talk about the characters they knew well as children. Why do you think that is?

Comic and cartoon characters – old favourites

People become very passionate about the media texts they enjoyed when they were young partly because they were so involved when they consumed them. Young children look forward eagerly for their favourite characters to come on television, or watch the video again and again, joining in with the words and actions. Choosing and buying their comic is an important part of their lives. Your childhood favourites become part of your identity. Try talking about your favourite Teenage Mutant Hero Turtles or Power Rangers from when you were younger – you may be surprised how much you still care!

ACTIVITY 1

1. For each character or series in the list below, discover:
   - when and where they first appeared
   - who created them
   - if they were used in more than one media form, e.g. a comic strip that became a TV series
   - whether they are still featured in new comic or TV stories.

   Use information from family and friends, old comics and videos, or a search engine on the Internet.
   - Scooby Doo
   - Dan Dare
   - Care Bears
   - Noggin the Nog
   - Mickey Mouse
   - The Bash Street Kids
   - Tintin
   - The Magic Roundabout
2. Build up an information sheet or poster on one of the characters. If you can, include drawings of the character. Discuss your findings with the rest of the class.

1 Tintin

Why are people's memories of cartoon characters so strong? Childhood characters are created very deliberately for children to identify with and remember. In addition, as you have seen, they are often found in several media forms, such as comics, television series and films, and even as merchandise. For example, Winnie the Pooh, who started as a character in a book, has appeared in cartoon films, comic strips, computer games, a track on a CD and on various forms of merchandise: stationery, clothing, tableware, furniture, and many more. These are called **tie-ins** and **spin-offs**. Can you think of any other characters who appear in so many forms?

KEY TERMS

Spin-off merchandise that uses characters from a media text

Tie-in a media text that uses the characters, and possibly storyline, of a text in another form

Character type and function

Vladimir Propp suggested in 1928 that in any story there are only ever a limited number of character types, each of which had their own purpose in the narrative.

TIP

You can find out more about any of the films mentioned in this unit from Internet databases via Heinemann Hotlinks.

Propp's main character types	
Hero	The **central protagonist** of the narrative who drives it forward and has some kind of quest or mission to undertake in return for a reward. Traditionally male, e.g. Fireman Sam, but can be female in modern narratives, e.g. Mulan in Disney's *Mulan* (1998).
Heroine or Princess	Acts as a reward for the hero for succeeding in the quest. In older, more stereotypical narratives the heroine is a **passive** princess and female, e.g. Daphne in *Scooby Doo*. In modern narratives, the heroine can be more active and feisty, e.g. Jasmine in Disney's *Aladdin* (1992).
Villain	Seeks riches, glory and/or power, and also seeks to stop the hero from succeeding in the quest or mission, while presenting a genuine threat. They sometimes want the heroine for themselves. They can be male, e.g. Scar in Disney's *Lion King* (1994) or female, e.g. Cruella de Vil in *101 Dalmations* (1996).
Donor or Mentor	Gives the hero important information or equipment to help him (or her) in the quest. They are often represented as wise or as having special powers, but are not able to do the quest without the hero, e.g. Shredder in *Teenage Mutant Hero Turtles*.
Helper	Accompanies the hero for some or most of the journey of the quest, and can even help the hero to succeed, but cannot by themselves complete the quest, e.g. Jess the cat in *Postman Pat*.

You have to be flexible when you classify characters into these types. Some characters fulfil two, or even more, functions. For example, the Heroine could also be the Helper – April is the heroine in *Teenage Mutant Hero Turtles*, but she also comes to the aid of the turtles on numerous occasions. Other character types have also been described that are not included in the list above.

KEY TERMS

Central protagonist the main character around whom the narrative is centred

Passive not helping the narrative to move forward or aiding the hero

2 Lara Croft: princess, hero, villain, donor or helper?

One character type that Propp does not discuss is the Threshold Guardian or Messenger. This character can be male or female, and often appears for only part of the narrative. They do, however, have an essential part to play in the journey of the hero. They may give the hero special knowledge to help them to go on, or have some kind of power, e.g. the dragon in *Shrek* (2001) (see **4**). Messengers/threshold guardians can be good or evil characters. An example of an evil character is the Hydra in Disney's *Hercules* (1997), which presents Hercules with his first test in his mission to become a true hero. Can you think of other Threshold Guardian figures in comics, cartoons or animations? Try to analyse what their particular function is in the narrative.

3 A student created this character profile

4 The dragon from *Shrek* (2001)

Superheroes

Many cartoon stories in comics and films are centred on heroic deeds. Yet it is clear that there is a difference between a hero – who drives the narrative forward with a mission to accomplish – and a **superhero** who often has special powers to help him or her save the world! Superhero stories are often used as a way of exploring great human themes like good and evil, truth or justice and corruption, love and sacrifice, tragedy and triumph. Can you think of any who do not have superpowers? Why do you think that animation is a particularly good media genre for portraying superheroes?

ACTIVITY 3

1 If you were a superhero, what superpowers would you choose? Why?

2 Make notes on, or draw, the superhero you would be.

3 Explain how your superhero got their powers.

4 If you have time, make notes or draw the arch-villain who opposes your superhero.

Audiences love superheroes because through them they are able to:

- explore beyond the boundaries of human possibility
- engage with the conflict between good and evil
- enjoy exploring the 'dark side' of so many superheroes, e.g. Batman, Daredevil.

Marvel comics

Your favourite film superheroes will probably come from the many created by Marvel Comics. Marvel are well known for their colourful and dramatic superheroes, which include Spiderman, The Hulk, the Fantastic Four and The Silver Surfer.

5 The Incredible Hulk

The first Marvel comic was published in the US in 1939, introducing the Submariner. Many of the best known Marvel characters were created in the 1960s, starting with the Fantastic Four in 1961. The Incredible Hulk (1962) (**5**) – influenced by characters from the books *Frankenstein* and *Dr Jekyll and Mr Hyde* – and Spiderman (1963) soon followed. Already Marvel were using **intertextuality** to create the Marvel universe – characters would guest star in each other's comic strips.

By 1966 Marvel characters had their own animated series on TV, showing five different stories featuring Captain America, Ironman, Hulk, Thor and Submariner. In the 1970s not only did Marvel heroes feature in full-length films, but Marvel were asked to create comics based on popular films such as *Star Wars*.

Marvel Enterprises today owns the rights to over four thousand characters, used in comic books, films and video games. The success of several blockbuster superhero films in recent years has led to spin-offs such as the Marvel Superhero Top Trumps game the girls are playing in **6**.

6 Marvel characters appear in many toys and games

Marvel superheroes

Marvel superheroes often show certain characteristics:

● some kind of tragedy in their past for which they want revenge, e.g. The Hulk

● double identity, e.g. Superman

● some kind of change to their genetic make-up that gave them their superpowers, e.g. Spiderman.

ACTIVITY 4

1 Make factfiles on your favourite Marvel heroes and villains. Describe their powers, their personal history and their greatest adventures. Use books, comics and a search engine on the Internet. You could also talk to comic fans, or visit a comic supplier such as Forbidden Planet.

2 Now compare the comic and film versions of some well known superheroes, such as Superman, X-Men and The Incredible Hulk. List and discuss the main similarities and differences between the two treatments.

TIP

You could use your factfile to help you write pieces of analysis, or to create designs for new characters at pre-production or production standard.

Analysing openings

The way a cartoon or animation begins is very important in setting up its narrative, characters, setting, main themes and general mood. Marvel comics are the basis for many film adaptations. These films usually begin with a Marvel **ident** in the form of a comic strip of famous superheroes to show the audience the roots of the film's storyline. The opening sequence that follows may show some of these features:

● establishing shots to set location

● first appearance of the superhero (who may not appear in their superhero form)

● a sound track that establishes mood.

7 The S is the ident in Superman films

ACTIVITY 5

1 First read these notes that a student wrote about the opening to *Daredevil* (2003).

> ● Opening panning shot of skyscrapers zooms into individual 'braille' style lights which are then 'translated' into title credits. Could the hero be blind?
>
> ● The hero wears a dark red outfit with his face hidden. His mask is removed and we are shocked that he is 'revealed'.
>
> ● A flashback helps us to understand that he suffered tragedy as a child, but that he also received supersonic sonar hearing as a result of the accident.

2 Watch two or three more openings to films based on Marvel superheroes. Write down the most important points in notes like those above.

3 Share your ideas about the openings you have seen with the class. Make a class list of the important features of openings.

KEY TERM

Ident like a logo, an instantly recognisable feature of a film, character or company, e.g. the Hulk's green fists

Comic conventions

Although comic strips are not audio-visual texts, they follow many of the same rules of narrative in that they are constructed to be like the frozen frames of moving texts. They are like dynamic **storyboards** which combine words and pictures to create the impression of sound, movement and tension. They rely most of all on very complex reading skills on the part of the comic reader – reading comics is far from a waste of time!

KEY TERM

Storyboard key moments of a story shown using images and notes

Key moments

When you are making a storyboard for a comic strip, it is useful to remember Todorov's Narrative Theory (see page 20). This suggests five stages in any story:

1 Equilibrium: establish setting, characters and storyline.

2 Disruption of the equilibrium, perhaps by an oppositional character.

3 Recognition of the disruption (often the longest part).

4 An attempt to repair the disruption.

5 Reinstatement of the equilibrium.

Your storyboard will need at least one frame for each stage.

Emily and the dragon

Emily was sick of waiting around for a wimpy prince to come and ask for her hand in marriage, so she decided to find one for herself. She soon came upon a dragon who was singeing the top of a freckle-faced boy's head.

Being a resourceful princess, Emily set a trap for the dragon and then tricked him into following her.

'You're just a silly girl, and even though it's hardly worth it, I'm going to toast you to a crisp and have you for pudding!' boomed the dragon. Just then, the branches he was standing on gave way, and he fell down a very deep well, his fire put out once and for all.

Emily returned to the boy. 'What's your name?' she asked.

'Prince Matthew,' said the boy.

'That'll do nicely,' said Emily. 'Where do you live?'

'In Happy-Ever-After,' he replied.

'That'll do nicely too,' said Emily. And with that, she and Matthew rode off together to Happy-Ever-After.

8 The story of Emily and the Dragon

ACTIVITY 6

You are going to work in pairs to make a storyboard for the story in **8**. You can see an example of a student's storyboard in **9**.

1 Decide on the most important details of the story – you are going to tell the story in six to eight frames. Remember that the story must still make sense and control pace and tension.

2 Now make a storyboard to tell the story. Try to make sure that the meaning is clear. Show that some frames will be close-ups and some will be from further away.

3 Pass the storyboards around the class so that everyone can see them. Discuss the similarities and differences between the storyboards. Did any groups use other techniques as well as drawing the key moments? How did they help to improve the impact of the story?

9 A student's storyboard

You will have seen how important it is to choose moments that are rich with meaning and convey lots of information to the audience. Remember that comic readers are very good at reading not only the information in each frame, but also the information implied between frames. For example, if a character is shown in Place A in one frame and Place B in the next, the audience will understand that the character has travelled there without anything interesting happening.

Comic techniques

Reading comics is more complicated than it may seem. Not only does the reader have to read a combination of words and images, they also have to 'read' the spaces in between the frames. With so many things going on at once, it is not surprising that there are a few 'rules' (codes and conventions) to help the reader pick up the right clues about making meanings from comic texts. Look at the examples in **10**.

IT WAS GETTING LATE, AND DAVID STILL HADN'T FINISHED HIS HISTORY ESSAY...

Text boxes – small boxes of text that give details that would be hard to show in pictures alone. They are placed at the top or bottom of a frame, or underneath a frame (very common in comics aimed at young children).

Thought bubbles – like speech bubbles, but the words are placed in cloud-shaped bubbles to show what the character is thinking.

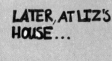

LATER, AT LIZ'S HOUSE...

Frame links – copy placed between frames to help the reader understand events which may have happened after the last frame and before the next one.

Speech bubbles – words of speech placed in a bubble pointing towards the mouth of the character who is speaking. Sometimes speech bubbles can point out of a frame to show that a character the reader cannot see is speaking.

10 Techniques used in comic strips

ACTIVITY 7

Split into teams of three or four people. Each team is given a range of comics aimed at different target audiences. See which group can find an example of every one of the comic techniques shown in **10** in the shortest time.

Sound words – Comics give the impression of sounds by using brilliantly inventive onomatopoeic words like 'POW!' and 'ZAPP!!'.

Emotion words – like sound words, comics also use words to show exactly how a character is feeling, e.g. 'BOOOOOOOOOOOOOORED!!!!'

Facial expressions – simple alterations to a character's face to show emotion.

Movement lines – comic frames are give the impression of movement by adding small lines around the edges of characters bodies and moving objects.

The best way to appreciate how sophisticated comic techniques are is to use them yourself. Follow the steps in Activity 8 to create a four- or five-frame photo-comic based on a famous fairy tale. Your aim is create a text which is eye-catching and easy to understand – you can see a good example in image **11**.

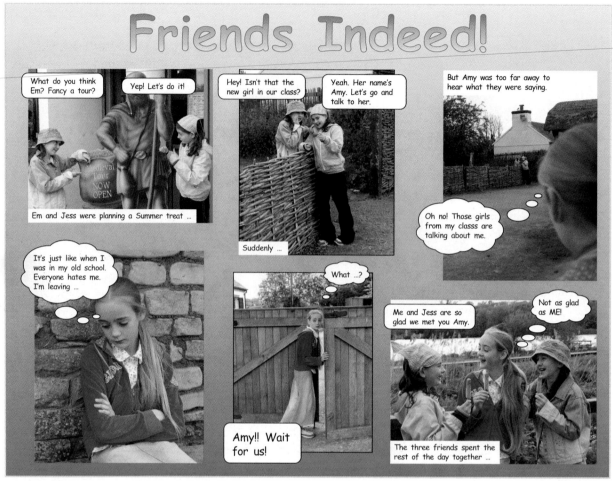

11 Some students put together this photo-comic for children under 10

ACTIVITY 8

1   Work in a group. Choose your story and decide on the age of your audience. Sketch the frames as a simple storyboard (see activity 6). Decide together how to take the shots.

2   Take the shots. Elaborate settings or costumes are not necessary since you can alter the photos using gel or correcting pens, by sticking things onto them or by cutting parts of them out. If you use a digital camera you can use a photo-editing package.

3   When your photos are ready, create your photo comic. You will need:
    • a large sheet of sugar paper
    • mounting paper for each photo
    • plain paper for writing or typing out text boxes and speech bubbles
    • an assortment of coloured pens etc. for decoration.

4   Give a group presentation to the rest of the class: show your photo-comic and explain how you created it and why. Alternatively, make a wall display: label your photo-comic to show how and why you made it the way you did.

Animation techniques

Several different techniques can be used to animate still images, each bringing their own unique style to the animation.

Line or cel drawing

This technique was used by the first animators. They drew a figure, framed in a background, many times, each time making tiny adjustments, and filmed each picture for just a frame or two. When the film was shown at normal speed the figure appeared to move.

ACTIVITY 9

Try creating your own simple animation. Think of a simple figure that you can draw, and choose a simple action, e.g. raising a hand to wave.

1   Draw the figure in the top right-hand corner of the first page of a small notebook.

2   On the second page draw the same figure with a slight change to show the beginning of the action.

3   On the next page, move the figure further, and so on until the action is completed.

4   Holding the notebook firmly in one hand, flick quickly through the pages with the other thumb so that you see your drawings in rapid succession. Your character will appear to move.

Computer-generated imagery (CGI)

It was obviously very time-consuming to draw so many frames. It took three years, for example, for the animators for Walt Disney's *Snow White* (1937) to complete their drawings. As early as the 1960s, people were working on ways to use computers to make the small adjustments to the original frame.

Since the early 1980s computers have been used in more and more sophisticated ways in animation. The first film to use **computer-generated imagery (CGI)** techniques was Disney's *Tron* (1983). The film was about a computer programmer (played by Jeff Bridges) who is sucked into his computer and turned into a 'virtual person' who must fight the main programme in order to survive. If you are able to see this film for yourself you will notice immediately how simple the technology is compared to that of today.

Now CGI allows whole worlds to be created and inhabited – sometimes without any human actors at all. Films entirely animated by computer include *Toy Story* (1995), *Final Fantasy: The Spirits Within* (2001) and *Shrek* (2001). What are your own favourite examples of film moments using CGI? Can you think of any moments when the technology works less well?

KEY TERM

Computer-generated imagery (CGI) any image or graphic generated or enhanced using a computer; used particularly for 3D special effects

ACTIVITY 10

Watch the opening of a film which uses a combination of CGI and real action, e.g. *Titanic* (1997). When does CGI work well and when does it not? Why?

ACTIVITY 11 EXTENSION

Watch the film *Simone* (2002) directed by Andrew Niccol. It explores the whole notion of using technology to create perfect computerised people or actors. It also raises some interesting points in relation to audiences and their adoration of stars.

Write a response to the film, offering your point of view about whether 'virtual actors' would work in reality or not, supported by references to moments from the film.

12 *Shrek* (2001) was entirely animated by computer

TIP

If you want to find out more about Ray Harryhausen and his influence on model animation technique, follow the links on the Heinemann Hotlinks site.

Model animation or stop-motion

Another successful and easy-to-recognise animation technique is **model animation**. A scale model of a character is moved and filmed in very small stages. This obviously takes a great deal of patience and time, and a camera that can film single frames in start-stop motion.

The technique was very popular in the 1960s and 1970s when Ray Harryhausen made model animation his speciality. He created characters such as the skeleton army in *Jason and the Argonauts* (1963), the goddess Kali in *The Golden Voyage of Sinbad* (1974) and Pegasus in *Clash of the Titans* (1980). This, his last film, took Harryhausen a year to create the effects and used 202 constructed shots.

13 A scene from the Harryhausen film *Jason and the Argonauts* (1963)

Other animators have used model animation since then, including Tim Burton in *The Nightmare Before Christmas* (1993). However, it was a young animator from Preston, Nick Park, who made model animation popular once more. In 1985 Nick joined Aardman Animations in Bristol and a few years later they introduced the world to Wallace and Gromit. The three short films became hugely popular with young and old alike, and won major acclaim including two Academy Awards. In 2000, Aardman produced the internationally successful *Chicken Run*, featuring the voices of Mel Gibson and Julia Sawalha, thus ensuring even further the popularity of model animation.

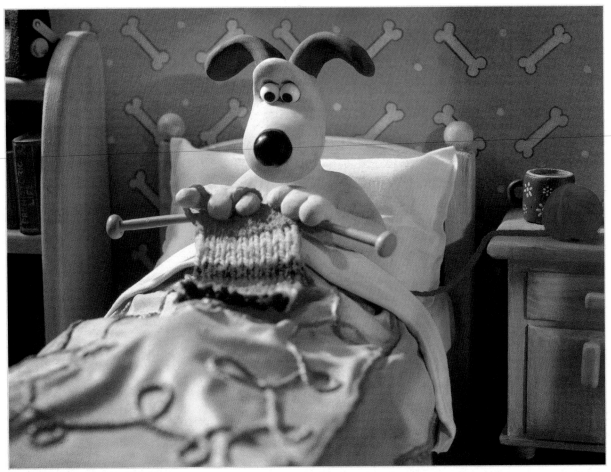

14 Gromit

ACTIVITY 12

Watch one or two scenes from Nick Park's animations. Try to spot how the animators have made the characters and settings as realistic and true to life as possible, e.g. Gromit raises his eyebrow to show his feelings, the wallpaper and pictures on the wall.

ACTIVITY 13 EXTENSION

If you have access to suitable technology, you could create your own simple model animation as a piece of coursework. Using either Plasticine or sheets of paper, make or draw a simple character. Work out a simple series of movements for the character to perform, and film each stage for 1–2 seconds. You need to record only about 1–2 minutes of footage.

Anime

Anime is a Japanese animation form which combines film-making with the **manga** comic form. Manga comics have been produced in Japan for many years, calling on the longstanding tradition of line art and Buddhist scrolls which had to be unrolled to reveal a message. They also used the Western tradition of telling stories in sequence, and the particular traditions of American comic books.

15 A manga comic strip

Anime directors are very interested in the effects of technology on society. The link to comics can be seen easily, since the intention of anime is to control the ways the viewer's eye looks at the screen. Many of the characters in anime are westernised, and some even look like early Disney characters.

Early anime animation leaned heavily on the idea of big comic frames (which were still) with large painted cels, but gave the impression of movement because the camera panned across them as it would in a film. The result was a semi-frozen animation, which emphasised angles and facial expressions, used tilt-ups and tilt-downs to give the impression of seeing more of a scene and zoom-ins to extreme close-ups to impress the audience.

Japanese animation is very concerned with meaning and symbolism. It draws attention to important details – since the frozen scene allows more time to look at everything – and gives clues about characters by their appearance. For example, large eyes suggest that characters are heroes or heroines, with good hearts and intentions. Small eyes suggest evil intent and usually belong to characters who are villains or villain's helpers.

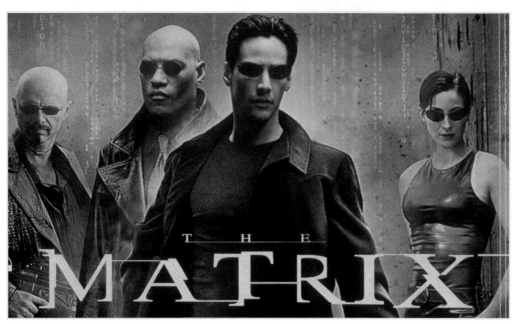

16 The Matrix trilogy was infleuenced by manga and anime

Some good examples of anime are *Akira* (1988) and *Ghost in the Shell* (1995). If you have the chance to see them, or any other anime films or cartoons, you will also notice how music and sound effects are used to create mood and atmosphere.

Many of you will have seen one or more of the Matrix trilogy (**16**), directed by the Wachowski brothers who acknowledge the strong influence of manga and anime on their film-making. They have also produced the *Animatrix* series of anime cartoons to accompany the films.

UNIT SUMMARY

Key area	What you have learned
Media language	• The different styles of animation • The language of comic codes and conventions • Features of superheroes
Audiences	• Who reads comics – not just small children • How audiences consume comics • Why audiences identify with superheroes
Institutions and organisations	• How comic and animation characters are used in spin-offs and tie-ins • The history of Marvel comics
Representation	• The functions of different character types • The role of the superhero

6 Pop music

In this unit you will find out:

- how pop music has many different genres with their own conventional features
- how audiences consume pop music in different ways
- how record companies and the music press market and publicise stars and their music
- how the stereotypical representations of pop stars are changing.

TALKING POINT

- Which bands and artists do you like? Talk about everyone's favourites.
- Did some people disagree fiercely with the choices of others? What different 'types' of music did you like?
- How many of the choices would you class as 'pop music'?

What is pop music?

You have just seen that young people tend to be passionate and protective of the bands and artists that they like. This could be because you spend a lot of time **consuming** your favourite tunes on television, the radio, portable CD-players and computers. The artists that you like may influence your opinions, your clothing or even how you see yourselves.

Pop music is one of the most popular media forms with teenagers today. New songs are targeted at them, and pop stars battle to become both the pin-up in their bedrooms and the voice on their minidisc players. Their parents despair at the sounds they hear pulsating through the floorboards, while music for them is one of the most popular media texts and the focus of many of their conversations with their friends.

1 Teenagers are avid consumers of pop music

Consuming the way that people take in a media text

Popular music music produced for a wide, mainly young, audience

Protest songs songs about issues, e.g. in the 1960s many American singers sang anti-war songs

So what exactly is pop music – not only typical pop music produced by manufactured boy and girl bands, but **popular music** as a whole? A definition of pop music could be: *any type of music having a wide appeal, that is, produced to be listened to by a large number of people.*

However, in your own lives popular music may play a wider role, shaping how you dress, how you talk and sometimes how you behave. Pop music is not just about the songs themselves but also about loyalty, fans, image and issues – all the things that teenagers are most interested in.

The lyrics of pop songs can influence the way people, especially young people, behave. In 2003, Culture Minister Kim Howells accused the So Solid Crew of 'glorifying gun culture and violence' and causing a rise in gun crime.

Lyrics can express feelings and topical social concerns, from anti-Vietnam war **protest songs** in the 1960s to hip-hop today. In 1970 Joni Mitchell, in *Big Yellow Taxi*, sang that:

> *They paved paradise*
> *And put up a parking lot …*

Take apart these lyrics and think of the meanings – what do you think that Mitchell was trying to say to the listener?

● Who do you think 'they' were?

● What was 'paradise'?

2 Joni Mitchell performing in San Francisco, 1977

Try to think of lyrics from current songs that comment on today's culture. Do singers still care about the same issues as Joni Mitchell did in 1970, or has the focus of songs changed over the years?

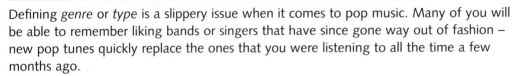

> ## ACTIVITY 1
>
> Watch a whole episode of *Top of the Pops*. Note down the bands and singers that feature on the programme.
>
> - In note form, summarise what each song is about. Which issues are being explored in the lyrics?
> - What does the selection reveal about current tastes, concerns and values?

Genres in pop music

Defining *genre* or *type* is a slippery issue when it comes to pop music. Many of you will be able to remember liking bands or singers that have since gone way out of fashion – new pop tunes quickly replace the ones that you were listening to all the time a few months ago.

Today, more and more people listen to and follow bands who do not make a great deal of money from their songs or reach a huge audience. These bands play **alternative** or **cult music**, meaning that it is popular largely because it is believed to be unpopular. In fact, many people believe that a band can only truly be described as 'alternative' if they are not liked by the mainstream audience. However, there have now been alternative bands in the charts – for example, Coldplay had a chart hit in 2002 with *Clocks*. The appeal of these bands is growing as many teenagers have become tired of commercial pop music and see alternative bands as having more 'street-cred'.

> ## ACTIVITY 2
>
> 1 Write down the title of the first pop music CD or tape that you remember listening to, and the last track or album you have bought. Are the genres of the two songs different? If so, try to think of reasons why.
> 2 Collate your findings onto a whole-class chart to see if there are clear winners – why are these tracks so popular?

Even from this brief look at genre, you should be able to see the huge spread of styles, bands and singers within the music industry. Sometimes even bands listed under a particular genre can be wildly different. Under the umbrella term of 'pop' there are many different sub-categories, ranging from Acid Jazz and Alternative to Worldbeat. As you can see from **3**, even the most obvious musical genres have deep roots and are not easy to pin down.

KEY TERM

Alternative or cult music songs that do not appeal to the usual pop audience

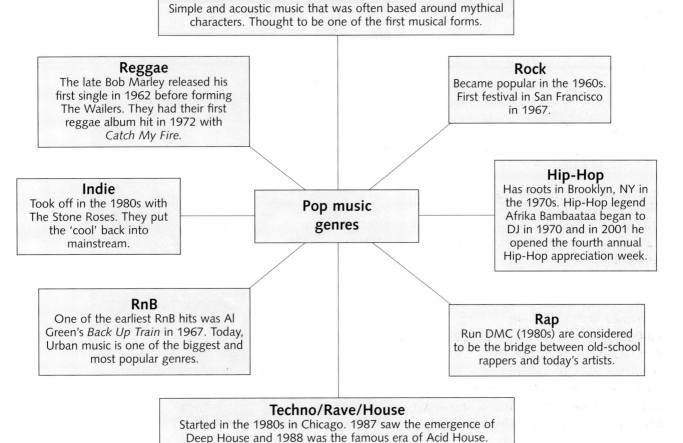

Folk
Simple and acoustic music that was often based around mythical characters. Thought to be one of the first musical forms.

Reggae
The late Bob Marley released his first single in 1962 before forming The Wailers. They had their first reggae album hit in 1972 with *Catch My Fire.*

Rock
Became popular in the 1960s. First festival in San Francisco in 1967.

Indie
Took off in the 1980s with The Stone Roses. They put the 'cool' back into mainstream.

Pop music genres

Hip-Hop
Has roots in Brooklyn, NY in the 1970s. Hip-Hop legend Afrika Bambaataa began to DJ in 1970 and in 2001 he opened the fourth annual Hip-Hop appreciation week.

RnB
One of the earliest RnB hits was Al Green's *Back Up Train* in 1967. Today, Urban music is one of the biggest and most popular genres.

Rap
Run DMC (1980s) are considered to be the bridge between old-school rappers and today's artists.

Techno/Rave/House
Started in the 1980s in Chicago. 1987 saw the emergence of Deep House and 1988 was the famous era of Acid House.

3 Some genres of pop music

Looking at genres in this way may prompt you to ask an age-old question about tastes – why are certain audiences attracted to music from some genres and not others? Perhaps they are influenced by their friends or by the geographical location they grew up in. Or perhaps they relate to a particular star and their lyrics seem relevant to their own lives. Try doing a survey of people from different audience groups to determine their music tastes and see if any patterns emerge. Use some of the categories on the spider diagram to help you think of questions about musical tastes and styles.

Genres are constantly being revisited or crossed until it is difficult to tell what genre some were originally meant to be. Just look at any music review page from a magazine and try to work out what they are saying about the genre of an artist: 'futuristic retro pop slashed with electro-pop'. Do you have any idea what this means?

The genre of music is important for music retailers and for young consumers. You may find that when you begin to analyse your own music consumption, you restrict yourself to a particular style or genre such as hip-hop or RnB. You may never move out of that particular section in your local music store (**4**).

ACTIVITY 3

Go into your nearest large music retail store and note down the categories that are available. These could range from Techno to Classical.

1 Does breaking the store down into these sections makes the music you want easier or harder to find?

2 Imagine that you are an artist with a new album to sell. Do you think that it would help you to have your music kept in a certain part of a music store? Make a list of pros and cons of the store layout for you as an artist.

4 Music retail stores: helpful sections or confusing?

Representation and the music press

The music press has huge influence when it comes to targeting audiences, and some magazines can influence current trends. Many teenagers read and talk about music magazines, and teenage magazines often have some form of music review pages. Magazines like *Mizz* and *Sugar* often feature chart music articles and contain interviews with stars that are considered to be the pop heart-throbs of the moment. Some of these magazines will concentrate on the **representation** and appearance of the star, indicating that the star's sex appeal is more important than their singing.

However, some of the music press will give detailed reviews of the music itself. Although entertainment magazines such as *Heat* review singles and albums, magazines such as *NME* (**5**) are seen as the main sources of opinion on the latest music trends.

These magazines are generally aimed at a youth audience as their features focus on the latest bands who may well be unknown to people from your parents' generation. They come out weekly and contain the most up-to-date reviews, interviews and gig information.

The *New Musical Express (NME)* (**5**) is one of the most established music magazines. It mainly features current bands and will often review alternative music. It is interesting to compare this magazine with a more mainstream pop magazine like *Top of the Pops* (**6**).

5 *NME* covers the alternative music scene

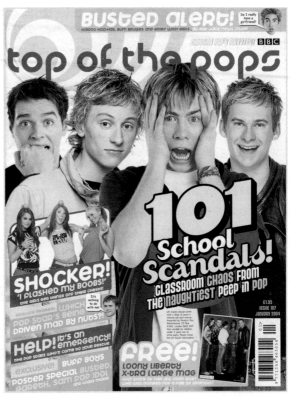

6 *Top of the Pops* is more mainstream – can you see any similarities?

ACTIVITY 4

Look at the covers of *NME* and *Top of the Pops* in **5** and **6**. Decide on a target audience for each magazine. Suggest ways that the content and layout of each magazine reach out to that audience. You may want to consider:

- the pop stars that are featured
- the **puffs** that say what is inside the magazine
- the design of the title block
- the colours used
- the price of the publication.

You could look back at pages 84–85 for help with analysing magazine covers.

© NME/IPC Syndication

KEY TERMS

Puffs text on the front cover that highlights some of the magazine's contents

Representation how the media present the 'real' world to us, e.g. how a pop star is made to look

Stereotypical how people expect a certain type of person to be represented

Of course, it is not just the covers of the magazines that are different – their contents vary as well. You have already seen how 'teen heartthrobs' are represented in magazines targeted at teenage girls.

There are other **stereotypical** representations to be found in the music press. Consider the ideas of the 'wild man of rock' such as Marilyn Manson and the 'independent diva' such as Beyonce Knowles. Publications such as *Kerrang!* rely on rock representations and the idea of the 'sex, drugs and rock and roll' lifestyle. The diva stereotype is more likely to be found in girl's magazines, such as *Glamour*. She is seen as a feisty and independent role model for the magazine's readers.

These representations offer more to their audiences than just a good read – they give the reader a chance to enjoy a relationship with a role model and gain information on their favourite star. The magazines know this and will represent the star in a stereotypical way, such as showing Marilyn Manson wearing make-up and dressed in black, glaring at the camera. These stereotypes reinforce what Manson's fans choose to believe about him – they enjoy his alternative representation and lifestyle and would not expect anything less from their favourite rock star. Because music magazines are becoming more popular all the time, there are now **fanzines** – magazines containing information, posters, song lyrics and interviews about one particular pop star.

ACTIVITY 5

1 Design an interview with a new music star for a music magazine that you know.

   • Write down the questions you would ask.

   • How could you **encode** the page with the features of the magazine to reflect the genre? For example, if the interview was for *Top of the Pops* you could use bright colours and ask questions about the star's love life (see **7** for an example).

2 Now put yourself in the place of the pop star. You need to decide on a particular representation for yourself – it should be as stereotypical as possible.

   • Make up some answers to the interview questions.

   • Take a photograph of yourself to include in the interview.

Describe the worst hairdo you've ever had.
Charlotte, Wolverhampton
Charlie: A bowl cut when I was about seven – I have nothing else to say!
Matt: When I was seven, I had hair that went out in enormous big ringlets – I hated it cos I looked like a girl and got called Piglet's Tail. So I cut my own hair one day at school, but then had bald patches everywhere! It ended up with my Auntie Val shaving all my hair off!
James: I had an appointment with the British Hairdresser of the Year and said, 'Do what you want!' But he gave me an off-centre mohican. I was like, 'I'd rather you shaved the lot off!'

Charlie, is it true you've got a girlfriend? Cos I'm gutted if you have!
Claire, Stockport
Erm, kind of. I'm thinking about seeing someone. I saw my ex-girlfriend the other day – so maybe, I don't know!

7 Put yourself in the place of Busted!

Of course, not all image representations are stereotypical, particularly now that the media are under pressure to stop showing stars as 'perfect'. Audiences are becoming tired of the stereotypical, glamorous pop star and 'ordinary' people are now selling records and making it to the coveted number one spot. Reality TV shows allow viewers to see people before they become stars and join them on their journey from first audition to first big hit. The public supported and voted for stars who did not always fit the typical star representation – singers like Alex Parks (see **8**), who won *Fame Academy* in 2003, broke the mould of the blonde, glamorous pop star.

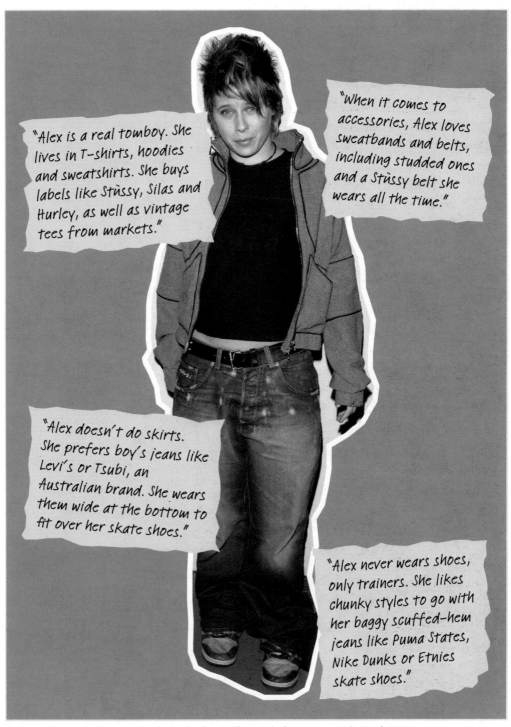

"Alex is a real tomboy. She lives in T-shirts, hoodies and sweatshirts. She buys labels like Stüssy, Silas and Hurley, as well as vintage tees from markets."

"When it comes to accessories, Alex loves sweatbands and belts, including studded ones and a Stüssy belt she wears all the time."

"Alex doesn't do skirts. She prefers boy's jeans like Levi's or Tsubi, an Australian brand. She wears them wide at the bottom to fit over her skate shoes."

"Alex never wears shoes, only trainers. She likes chunky styles to go with her baggy scuffed-hem jeans like Puma States, Nike Dunks or Etnies skate shoes."

8 Singer Alex Parks is represented as a tomboy in this article from *CosmoGirl!*, March 2004

Michelle McManus, who won *Pop Idol* during 2003, is another mould-breaker. A size 20 singer, she fought against the stereotypical representation of pop image to win the competition.

KEY TERM

Anchorage text text, often a caption, that goes with a picture and 'anchors' the readers' interpretation of the image

- Look at the cover of *Heat* magazine celebrating her win (**9**). The **anchorage text** says how she 'bravely overcame weight insults'. This shows how the public supported the star, even when the judges of the show criticised her appearance.

- In the interview inside the magazine, *Heat* describes how she brought 'a breath of fresh air to the pop world of skinny girlbands and cheesy boybands'.

Perhaps pop representations are changing. Are pop audiences becoming more concerned with the music itself than with the appearance of the star? Michelle's success may also lessen pressure on large girls to conform to the skinny stereotypes that have been favoured in the media. Ask around your classroom to get different opinions on what makes a pop star – how many people mention appearance?

J-Lo's Christmas ruined by killer flu!

This week's hottest celebrity news
£1.45 (Canary Islands €3.00; Spain €2.70) 3 – 9 January 2004

heat

MAGAZINE OF THE YEAR!

Pop Idol

HUNGOVER? Us too. Celebs offer their detox tips

PLUS

RICKY GERVAIS PICKS HIS FAVOURITE POP IDOL MOMENT!

"I can't believe it!" **Michelle!**

IN HER **FIRST MAJOR INTERVIEW**
MICHELLE TALKS ABOUT WINNING –
AND HOW SHE BRAVELY
OVERCAME WEIGHT INSULTS

Issue 251

THEY'RE COUNTING THE WEEKS!
LOOK AT THEIR BABY BUMPS!

9 *Heat* magazine, 3–9 January 2004

Manufactured pop – talent or trash?

How many manufactured bands and singers can you think of? Some examples have already been mentioned. How many of them started off as part of the TV Pop phenomenon? Are you surprised at how many of these stars came from TV shows? Television shows are often used to kick-start the careers of many hopeful singers and sell as many singles as possible.

The huge success of shows such as *Popstars*, *Pop Idol*, *Pop Stars: The Rivals* and *Fame Academy* proves that **voyeuristic** or reality TV is certainly easy to watch. Saturday night television suddenly became primetime viewing as thousands of teenagers phoned or texted to vote for their favourite Pop Idol.

However, after choosing the winner, did they really care about what happened to the band after the programme had finished? Groups like Hear'say and One True Voice were launched into mega-stardom very quickly, but now, at car boot sales all over the country, you can buy their assorted **memorabilia** for next to nothing.

10 The Backstreet Boys

11 Blue

ACTIVITY 6

Look at some examples of different boy bands (see **10**, **11**) and listen to some of their tracks. Use the following questions to help you analyse what you see and hear.

1   Is there a formula for these bands? For example, are there certain types always included: the cute one, the tough one, etc.?

2   Listen to tracks by different boy band artists. Are there similarities between style of music and type of song?

3   Who are the target audience for these bands? What features appeal to the target audience?

Success stories such as Will Young, Gareth Gates and David Sneddon have taught us that new 'television pop stars' are guaranteed instant fame. During Christmas 2003, the only two contenders for the coveted Christmas Number One spot were Girls Aloud and One True Voice, both the pop star inventions of TV pop shows. The shows that led up to the launch of the new stars are known as **tie-ins**. This is because the show helps to publicise them and the single they were to release.

The added media attention on the television programme lets the audience see what all the contestants are really like, making them seem more human to them.

ACTIVITY 7

Try to create your own new boy/girl band. You could use friends or members of your class, create pop star identities for them and photograph them in role. Once you have decided upon their star type and their representation, the possibilities are endless – you could plan magazine interview pages and reviews, or storyboard a video.

Manufactured bands – the end of the road?

Hear'say, the first manufactured band to come out of a TV show, split less than two years after entering the limelight. This could suggest that manufactured bands quickly reached their peak and that listeners got tired of them. David Sneddon announced, just one year after winning *Fame Academy* in 2002, that he would rather write songs for other people than stay in the limelight himself.

James Oldham, deputy editor of *NME*, gave his opinion on TV-assisted pop in 2003:

> I think there will always be plastic, manufactured groups around, but there has definitely been a shift in attitude over the last 12 months … labels are investing more and more in signing up new bands as opposed to commercial pop groups. The 'Popstars' format will eventually die.

Have a look at a recent chart list. How much of the Top Ten is made up of manufactured pop? Is James Oldham right?

Bands with staying power

ACTIVITY 8

Conduct some Internet research into the best-selling albums of all time. You can find useful information via Heinemann Hotlinks. Try to print out a list. Are there any manufactured or TV pop bands on the list? Does it surprise you that there are so few modern artists in the list?

Do you think that there is a person on the planet who has not heard of the Beatles? Albums by bands like the Beatles and Led Zeppelin (**12**) continue to sell in significant numbers, even though the bands are no longer together, and some band members have died.

Record companies have begun to recognise that, while manufactured groups can make them a quick profit, they do not have the staying power of 'real' bands. Big names such as Universal, the largest record company in the UK with 40 per cent of sales, are investing massively in signing up new 'real' bands for this reason.

12 The Beatles and Led Zepellin – still selling

It would be interesting to know what you will all be listening to in ten years' time. Will you still listen to manufactured pop bands, or will you be enjoying classics like Stevie Wonder or Bob Dylan? Perhaps there is no real love or passion for music amongst TV pop groups, and that is why so many modern pop songs sample old hits.

When introducing rock band The Darkness on their first appearance on *Top of the Pops* in October 2003, Richard Bacon said that their success 'raised two fingers at manufactured bands'. Their debut album went double-platinum and enjoyed three weeks at the top of the album chart in 2003, suggesting that young people soon got tired of being spoonfed 'poptastic' tunes.

ACTIVITY 9

Stage a class debate about manufactured bands. Half of the class should find reasons why manufactured groups deserve a place in the charts; the other half find arguments against the idea.

Ownership and control – the industry

Pop music first became big business with rock and roll in the 1950s. Stars like Elvis Presley were originally signed to independent companies like Sun Records, but the big companies soon snapped them up when they started to become more famous. By 1973, the major record companies controlled over 80 per cent of the music market.

As you saw earlier, Universal is the largest record company in the UK. Four other major companies dominate the music market today – Sony Music Entertainment, Warner Music International, EMI and BMG. These global companies are always looking for stars or pop personalities who would appeal to an audience.

Independent record companies are popular with lots of new bands today because they are seen as more innovative and more in touch with young audiences. Sometimes the big companies are seen as being cunning or manipulative and just out for a quick profit. However, major companies and independent labels are often one and the same thing today, with the big companies buying smaller ones out when they become successful. They then work together to develop new artists.

ACTIVITY 10

Find out more about the links between major record companies and the independents.

1   Look at CD covers or in magazines like *NME* that review alternative music. How many independent record companies can you spot? Make a list of some that have popular bands or singers signed to them.

2   Try to find out if any of these 'independent' companies are linked to the big businesses. You can do this by accessing the websites of the major record companies and searching for the companies they own.

There are a few key roles in a record company, supported by others. One of the main roles is the **A and R manager**, whose responsibilities include scouting talent and signing bands. The A and R manager works closely with the *marketing manager*, who develops plans to market the star or the band and decides on a star's image. There is also a *promotions manager*, a *press officer*, a *label manager* and a *video commissioner*. Large companies will also have a team in charge of *distribution*, which handles the company's sales in stores and on the Internet.

What if you wanted to start your own independent label today? It would be no small task! You would need to:

- decide upon a genre of music for your label

- do market research on the audience for that genre

- provide details and promotional information for the bands you had signed

- contact distribution companies that deal with your genre of music, including those that distribute over the Internet.

Music from the Internet: illegal downloading

Today, record companies are fighting a war against downloading music from the Internet. This is a really important issue for record companies and is linked to the issue of copyright. Copyright brings in about a third of a record company's profits, so companies are obviously keen to enforce laws that stop people illegally downloading or copying songs. The battle against copyright infringement goes back as far as the 1980s when companies became worried about people recording songs onto blank cassettes.

The battle today is even bigger and harder to control. Industry sales fell by 22 per cent between 1999 and 2000 because of single file-sharing, and record companies complained about the rise of the 'one-hit wonder'. Only singles sold, but record companies earn most of their money from albums. Albums turn 'bands into brands', with the power of **spin-offs** allowing cash to be made from T-shirts and calendars. Money can also be generated from tie-ins such as tours or TV shows.

> ### ACTIVITY 11
> List some ideas for merchandise and spin-offs that could be created for a band or a singer. Try to come up with some really original ideas.

File-sharing: the companies fight back

The companies are fighting back, however. The Recording Industry Association of America (RIAA) took the Internet site Napster to court in 2000, over their music file-sharing system. In 2001, Napster was found guilty, forced to shut down and invent a new pay-for-download system. Their new site contains the Visa and Mastercard logos.

In 2004, the RIAA sued 914 Americans for millions of dollars for uploading songs. These people were using software packages KaZaA and BearShare to file-share songs. One of the accused was a 12-year-old girl. Her mother settled out of court by paying the RIAA US $2000, and thousands of American families banned their children from using file-sharing sites.

Record companies have been forced to admit that digital music is the future, but they want it done legally. They have hired computer experts to dump corrupted files onto sites, so that users have to search around for hours to find the track they were looking for. Madonna even circulated fake tracks from her 2003 album *American Life* – fans who tried to download songs were met with silence and an angry message from 'Madge' herself asking what they thought they were doing!

David Munns, the vice-chairman of EMI, has likened file-sharing to going into a music store and shoplifting CDs. However, figures from research companies still suggest that at any given time there are up to five million people illegally sharing songs worldwide.

Stars and their fans

Pop music is a source of endless pleasure for its listeners, who in return give tremendous loyalty to the stars they listen to. Established stars like Madonna and Kylie can withstand criticism and gossip, because fans will support and admire them, whatever they do.

Becoming a fan takes time. You may start off by hearing a song and liking it for its tune or because the lyrics link to something in your own life. Then you may start to feel some sort of identification with the star. Next you begin to buy all the albums by that star, even **back catalogues**, memorabilia and possibly other merchandise as well. This is all normal behaviour for a fan!

Fan clubs now have record numbers of members, fanzines are becoming more and more popular and some fans go as far as to dress like their idols. At its most extreme this can result in Elvis lookalike competitions.

KEY TERMS

Back catalogue past albums from a particular star, not their latest hit

Mise-en-scene the 'putting together' of a scene, including props, setting, colour, lighting, facial expression and so on

13 Elvis performing in 1977

Stars with staying power

So what gives a star staying power? Most groups and singers come and go, and the charts are full of 'one-hit wonders'. You may love these songs at the time and even buy the single, but how often do you like the artist enough to purchase the whole album?

However, there are some stars who stand the test of time and manage to reinvent their image in order to stay at the top of the charts. Kylie Minogue, for example, had seven number ones in the UK between 1988 and 2003. Her seventh number one single *Slow* sold 48 500 copies in the first week it was released. The track made Kylie the female artist with the longest span of number one singles, with fifteen years and seven months between *I Should Be So Lucky* (her debut single) and *Slow*.

What makes Kylie still a hit with you today, when people much older than you can remember listening to her when *they* were in school? Perhaps in the first place it was her ability to reinvent her image from the girl-next-door from *Neighbours* that everyone loved to glamorous international star (**14**). Her record company, EMI, certainly provided her with a new look and some winning singles for her more recent albums. Her appeal then reached to a wider audience, attracting fans from both genders, instead of just teenage girls.

TIP

This could become an interesting piece of coursework. (You can find older videos on the Internet ... or at car boot sales!)

14 The changing faces of Kylie Minogue, 1993–2003

Marketing the music

A song can be outstanding, and the performers sensational, but if no one knows about it, no one will buy it. Another issue linked to stars and their record companies is how the stars and their records are promoted.

Start by looking at the charts. Every week, all over the world, charts naming the best-selling singles and albums are compiled by a company called Gallup and published in the music press. No one in the industry would deny the importance of the charts, because selling records is how the companies make their money.

Getting a record into the charts brings it to the attention of the public. It gets air-play on the radio and in pubs and clubs. Once a single is seen to be popular, more people want to buy it! This explains why record companies invest so much time and money on **marketing** a pop record before it gets released.

Once the record has been marketed, it is distributed. A large record company will have their own **distribution** department who will ensure that their signings have pride of place in record stores and on Internet sites. Smaller companies may have to approach individual distribution companies to handle their albums and singles.

ACTIVITY 15

Look out for the release of a new single by a well known singer or band. The advertising and promotion before its release might involve posters, TV appearances, radio or magazine interviews, and newspaper reviews.

1 Keep a log of all the marketing activity you see related to the single. Try to answer these questions:

- Do the artists appear on TV?
- Are they interviewed on the radio?
- Are any other forms of advertising used?
- How long does it take for the music press to pick up on the release?
- Is the record linked with any other media product, e.g. the soundtrack to a new film?

2 Once the single has been released, track its position in the charts, writing in your log the highest position it reaches and how long it stays inside the Top Twenty.

KEY TERMS

Distribution making the record available for sale in high street stores and on the Internet

Marketing advertising and promoting a product

Sometimes singles by more than one well known star come out in the same week, and the publicity machine goes into overdrive. However, when this happens, no one loses out because the record sales of *all* of the artists are boosted as their latest singles and albums fly off the shelves.

ACTIVITY 16

Design your own CD cover for a new band or artist that is about to be marketed and promoted by their record company. The CD can be from any musical genre. Make sure that you carefully consider the front and back covers, as well as the spine. Include the **conventions** of CD covers. These include:

- the name of the band
- the name of the album
- a lyric list
- a spine, showing the band and album name
- a barcode
- **production details**.

If you are particularly artistic, this could be drawn, but otherwise, create your cover using a PC. You could use images from the Internet and even find a barcode to copy onto it.

KEY TERMS

Conventions features that often appear on a certain type of media text

Multi-tracking where different voices and instruments are recorded separately and then mixed in a studio

Production details the small print, such as dates, copyright symbols, company names, etc.

15 Media Studies students designed these CD covers

Technology and the future of pop

In the beginning there was live music. The rich were able to hire musicians to play in their homes, but, except for singing or playing themselves, poorer people had to find a place where it was being played and listen outside.

The most important date in the music industry is 1877 when Thomas Alva Edison invented the world's first recording machine. Twelve years later, recordings were available for the public.

Originally, music was recorded on wax cylinders. Later 78 rpm (revolutions per minute) discs were played on a clockwork player that had to be wound up to make the record go around. A steel needle was placed onto the record; this had to be changed regularly as it wore down quickly.

A major breakthrough for music technology came in the 1940s when Les Paul began experimenting with 'sound-on-sound' recording, which is known today as **multi-tracking**. It involved laying down one basic track and then adding more tracks, one after another. This made it possible for just one man to produce a track with many instruments on it.

Multi-tracking is now used in all recordings, which is why artists often sound very different live than they do on their albums. It is very easy for a sound engineer to manipulate the track so that the recording is not a true representation of what was being sung at the time.

Today, of course, music can be heard in many different ways. You can spend thousands of pounds on state-of-the-art, surround-sound CD/DVD/MD/MP3 players, or even listen to the radio through your mobile phone.

ACTIVITY 17

Make a list of all the different places you hear music in one week. Include the times when you were:

- a **primary consumer** who deliberately listened to something
- a **secondary consumer**, letting the music stay in the background – listen out carefully for this or you might just miss it.

As you can see from Activity 17, you are now surrounded by music. Music and the technology linked to it have changed hugely over the past 75 years. Devices such as the Apple iPod are seen as the biggest revolution in music since the Walkman. This type of device allows users to store thousands of songs straight onto it from their computers – Apple's iTunes online music store sold 30 million singles in America in 2003.

ACTIVITY 18

Create a playlist for a chosen target audience.

- If possible, use a PC to download suitable tracks onto the hard drive and put together your own playlist.
- Include an evaluation justifying all your choices and saying why they would appeal to the audience you have chosen. Use the Uses and Gratifications theory (see page 88) in your justification.

You have already looked at the effect that this increasingly new technology might have on the future of the record companies. They will certainly have to adapt if they are going to keep up with the fast pace of the technological advances. In early 2004, legal sales of singles over the Internet overtook sales of singles in the shops. Companies are now trying to make deals with Internet sites, and prosecuting uploaders in 2004 helped sales to pick up in the industry. Cut-price CDs have also helped the record companies to make a comeback.

KEY TERMS

Primary consumer someone who is absolutely focused on a media text

Secondary consumer someone who is watching, listening to or reading a media text while doing something else

ACTIVITY 19

Hold a class discussion about the pros and cons of using the Internet to download music. Consider the statement below:

As the Internet becomes available to more and more people, CD sales will continue to fall and artists seeking publicity will use the Internet as their sole means of distribution.

The pop music video

Start to review your own pop video history by thinking of your top three favourite videos and why you like them. Is it because you particularly like the star, or does the video have certain elements that you enjoy? Are there any videos that were chosen by several people in the class?

A hit single is no longer enough on its own. This is a visual age, and pop fans love a pop video as much as the single itself. Think about the videos you chose just now. Probably many of your favourites were chosen because they are sensational or funny. The important things are that the video sticks in your heads and that it can be watched again and again without you getting bored.

Videos are also important in enabling viewers to visualise a star. They create an image for the singer, which can then develop over time, as you have already seen with Kylie.

Pop videos can also be seen as a three-minute piece of modern art that is used to sell the singer and the single. This is why some music artists work with Hollywood directors on their videos, for example Michael Jackson worked with Hollywood director John Landis on his *Thriller* video (see **16**).

16 A scene from Michael Jackson's *Thriller* video

ACTIVITY 20

Watch a selection of pop videos. You can find current pop videos on the Internet by using www.heinemann.co.uk/hotlinks. For each one:

- sum up what the video is trying to tell us about the artist
- explain what sort of audience you think the video is trying to appeal to.

UNIT SUMMARY

Key area	What you have learned
Media language	• Pop music has many sub-genres, such as hip-hop and reggae. • How to read the mise-en-scene of a music video to analyse a pop star.
Audiences	• How the Uses and Gratification theory can be used to show why audiences enjoy certain songs. • How audiences are influenced by the music press. • How audiences consume music in different ways.
Institutions	• How record companies use spin-offs and tie-ins to promote records. • How the music industry is dominated by a small number of major companies. • How the industry has suffered because of the Internet. • How the industry markets and promotes its stars.
Representations	• How representations of music stars are often linked to stereotypes. • How the music press relies on stereotypical images of pop stars to capture their target audience. • How these stereotypes are changing. • How pop videos help to establish a star's image.

7 Radio

In this unit you will find out:

- how music, speech and sound effects are used by a radio station to create a recognisable house style
- how radio stations research and target their audiences
- how BBC and commercial radio stations are funded, and how this affects their schedules and content
- how radio stations choose news items.

TALKING POINT

Talk about the answers to these questions in a group of three or four. Make notes of the decisions your group has come to.

1 How important is each of these in your life: TV, newspapers, magazines, radio? Put them into a rank order as a result of your discussion.

2 When do you listen to the radio?
- In bed at night
- Radio alarm when waking up
- At school
- Having breakfast
- While doing homework on a computer
- While playing video/computer games
- Preparing to go to school

3 Where do you listen to the radio?
- Bathroom
- Kitchen
- Car
- Other places, such as ...?
- Living room
- Bedroom
- School

Couch potatoes or what?

Some reports say that you and your friends do little else but sit around watching telly and eating endless packets of crisps, bars of chocolate and gallons of fizzy drink. Your generation is the ultimate bunch of couch potatoes, they say.

That is what is called a **stereotype**. Of course, in reality you and your friends are a group of individuals who have similar interests but very different personalities and habits.

Leaving out the junk food, concentrate on what the professionals would call your **media consumption**. A bit like food, you 'take in' all sorts of different media forms each day. Some of them you take in deliberately – like sitting down to read a magazine. Others you take in because there is no escape – like seeing a poster for the latest Hollywood action movie splashed across the bus shelter on your way to school.

Television usually gets all the bad press about turning you into 'brain-dead zombies'. Have you ever heard anyone say: 'They just spend all their time sitting round listening to the *radio?*' So – do you? What did your group discussion show?

KEY TERMS

Stereotype shared characteristics given to a group of people

Media consumption the media texts you watch, listen to or read

The questions you answered came from a survey specially conducted by the radio industry. Now compare your findings with the answers given by people aged 16–34. Are any of the graphs very different from your own answers? Is there anything that you find surprising?

Question 1: How important is each of these in your life: TV, newspapers, magazines, radio?

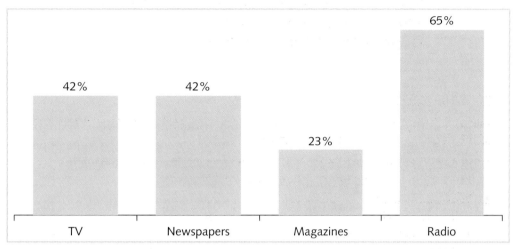

1 Percentages of 16- to 34-year-olds who say that each media form is an important part of their lives

Conclusion of the research: Radio plays a more important role in the daily lives of young people than television or the press.

Question 2: When do you listen to the radio?

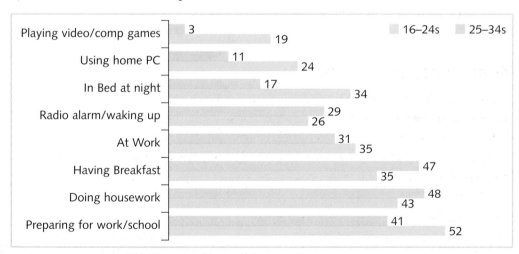

2 When 16- to 34-year-olds listen to the radio (percentages)

Conclusions of the research: Young people use radio to accompany them throughout the day, tuning in while they get ready in the mornings, during breakfast and while doing household chores. Listening at work is also popular within this age group, especially amongst 16–24-year-olds.

Younger audiences also use the radio to relax – while using the home PC, playing video/computer games or simply in bed at night.

Question 3: Where do you listen to the radio?

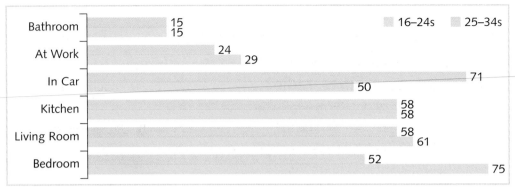

| | 16–24s | 25–34s |

- Bathroom: 15 / 15
- At Work: 24 / 29
- In Car: 71 / 50
- Kitchen: 58 / 58
- Living Room: 58 / 61
- Bedroom: 52 / 75

3 Where 16- to 34-year-olds listen to the radio (percentages)

Conclusion of the research: As lifestyles within the 16–34 age group vary, so do the ways in which radio is consumed. For example, listening while driving is more popular amongst the 25–34-year-olds – younger respondents are less likely to have the opportunity to do so.

With many people in this age group still living at home or sharing with friends, the bedroom is an important personal space for young people: 75 per cent of 16–24-year-olds listen to the radio in their bedrooms.

Why do people listen to the radio?

The results of the survey show that people listen to the radio under many different circumstances. Why do people choose to put the radio on? The Uses and Gratifications Theory (see page 88) can be used to show that people consume media texts to satisfy a variety of needs:

- The need to be INFORMED and EDUCATED about the world
- The need to IDENTIFY with characters and situations to learn more about ourselves
- The need to be ENTERTAINED
- The need to use the media as a talking point for SOCIAL INTERACTION
- The need to ESCAPE from our 'daily grind' into other worlds and situations.

ACTIVITY 1

Work in your group again.

1   Talk about how you use the radio to satisfy the needs listed above.
2   Which needs does each radio station you mentioned in your discussion fulfil? Give each one a score between 1 and 10 for each need:

TIP

Use a mnemonic to help you remember the five needs in the Uses and Gratifications Theory, e.g.
I immensely enjoy sending emails.

A short history of radio in the UK

1922	British Broadcasting Corporation licensed to transmit radio programmes.
1928	Radio audience of over 1 million.
1933	First commercial radio – Radio Luxembourg broadcasts popular music programmes on an unauthorised frequency.
1939	Nine million radios in the UK: most people listen to the Prime Minister, Neville Chamberlain, announcing war with Germany.
1947	First portable 'transistor' radios.
1958	Radio audiences dwindle as audiences for TV dramatically increase: BBC Radio's evening audience is down to 3.5 million.
1964	'Pirate' radio stations playing modern pop music start to broadcast to the UK from ships offshore, outside the broadcasting law. They attract large audiences of young people.
1967	Pirate radios closed down by law. The BBC opens pop station Radio 1.
1967	BBC Leicester, first BBC Local Radio station, opens.
1973	First legal commercial radio stations open: Capital Radio and LBC in London.
1980–2000	An increasing number of radio stations receive licences.
TODAY	There are seven BBC national network stations (Radios 1–5, World Service and Asian Network UK), 41 BBC local radio stations, ten national commercial radio stations, 207 local commercial stations and large numbers of community radio stations.

4 People listened to radios like this in the 1930s

5 A modern hi-tech radio station

What makes radio stations different?

Funding: Beeb versus the rest

So what is the difference between a BBC radio station and a commercial radio station? The answer is very simple – who pays the bills.

The BBC gets the money to run its radio and television channels from a yearly payment called the *licence fee* (£114 in 2004) from everyone who owns a TV. The BBC is called a *public service broadcaster* because they are funded by the public. Although the BBC makes some money through selling their programmes, books and other merchandise, the public pay the largest part of the bill. So, no licence fee – no BBC.

Commercial radio has to cover its running costs by attracting advertisers who pay to market their products or services on air. No adverts – no commercial radio – or commercial TV! You can find out more about how radio advertising works on pages 162–163.

Talk versus music

Radio stations can also be divided into those that predominantly play music and those whose output is much more speech-based. BBC Radios 1, 2 and 3 and most commercial radio stations base their programmes around music. There is some speech – presenters talk between records, newsreaders give updates and weather forecasts – but the majority of air time is taken up by music. In contrast, BBC stations like Radio 5 Live and Radio 4 are almost all speech-based, so that if you tune in to them at any time of day or night you are much more likely to hear people talking than music.

Sounding you out

Compared with television, radio is beautifully simple to produce. Although a great deal of thought may have gone into the sounds that come out of your radio and a team of people involved to get them 'on air', there are only three ingredients that programme producers can mix together:

- the human voice
- music
- sound effects.

But those three simple ingredients can certainly be made to sound very different indeed. The look of a big-name trainer is about creating **brand awareness**. The sound of a radio station is also to do with **branding**. How many radio stations can you recognise the instant you hear them? It is vitally important for a station to create their own sound or **house style** because this will be the sound that they know their audience like.

The most important feature of a house style is the way the presenters talk to their audience. You know from your own experience that the way you speak to people depends on who they are and what the situation is. If you are caught breaking a school rule, the language and style you use when you tell a friend what happened are very different from those you use to a teacher. Radio presenters adapt the way they speak to suit the audience they think will be listening. Their job is to build up a relationship with each listener, to keep them listening to the station and – vitally important – to get them to tune in on a regular basis.

KEY TERMS

Brand awareness Making the product immediately recognisable to the public

Branding a unique 'personality' for the product

House style a particular sound that matches the people who listen to the station

People who run radio stations often talk about presenters who have a 'good voice for radio'. This is a bit vague, but in his book *Broadcast Journalism*: *Techniques of Radio and TV News*, writer and broadcaster Andrew Boyd described a 'good microphone voice' as one that is 'reasonably rich, crisp and resonant and free from obvious impediments'. In contrast a voice that is 'piping, reedy, nasal, sibilant, indistinct or very young-sounding' would not work so well.

There are other factors that presenters must think about when presenting their programmes. The **tone** they adopt will be crucial. You could use any of the words in **6** to describe the tone of a presenter's voice:

serious	light-hearted	assertive	calm
scathing	soothing	humorous	pompous
aggressive	solemn	mocking	contemptuous
intimate	patronising	chatty	over-excited

6 Words that describe tone

ACTIVITY 2

1   Look up any of the words in Boyd's descriptions that you do not understand. With a partner, discuss the voices of the various teachers you work with. Using Boyd's definition, decide which one you think has the best radio voice and whose voice might work least well on radio.

2   Choose which terms in **6** apply to the two voices you have chosen.

How would you describe the tone of voice used by the radio presenters you listen to most frequently? The tone they use will affect the way they come across to their listeners. Some programmes will want to sound friendly, as if the presenter is talking to their friends. Others will be more formal, providing a 'voice of authority' on whatever it is they are discussing.

Another consideration will be the **pace** at which they talk – is it very slow and measured or is it rapid and quick-fire?

Finally, there will be the **accent** of the presenter's voice. At one time the BBC expected all its presenters to speak in *received pronunciation*, which was seen as a Southern, slightly posh way of speaking. Now it uses presenters who talk in a range of regional accents, reflecting the rich and diverse backgrounds its listeners across the country are coming from.

ACTIVITY 3

You are going to research the style and content of these radio stations:

- BBC Radio 1 • BBC Radio 4 • Your local commercial radio station
- A radio station broadcasting in a foreign language.

1 Listen to the sound of each station. Use a grid like the one below to make notes of your findings so that you can discuss them with others afterwards:

- *Presenters' voices:* use the ideas outlined on the previous page to help you make detailed notes about the style of the presenter's voice.
- *Programme content:* describe the type of music played or the subject being broadcast by speech-based programmes.

Radio station	Presenter's voice	Programme content
BBC Radio 1		

TIP

Presenting information as a chart or table will save you time in your exam.

2 Discuss your notes with a partner. Try to decide which type of listener you think each station is targeting with its house style.

Making the link

Chatting for 30 to 40 seconds and then playing a record may not seem like hard or difficult work, but making it sound that easy is the sign of a good presenter. Remember, most radio goes out live. Presenters try to make it sound as if what they are saying has just popped into their heads, as it would in a conversation with another person.

Some stations follow American research which suggests that presenters prepare their **links** by following these steps:

1 Choose an idea or topic which will interest or amuse your listener.

2 Brainstorm anything you can think of saying about that topic onto paper.

3 Choose one strong idea from your brainstorm and write an interesting first sentence which will hook your listeners into the link.

4 Identify two further ideas you will use to develop the topic.

5 Write a really strong sentence to end the piece (sometimes called a *power out*).

6 Make it sound unscripted when you actually do the piece live on air.

ACTIVITY 4

1 Record two links from a local radio station: one with just a single presenter talking and the other with two presenters talking to each other.

2 Play these back and make a written transcript of exactly what is said.

3 Discuss with a partner whether you think either link seems to have used the American approach.

4 Now try it yourself! Write a script for a 40-second link on any topic of your choice using the six steps. Swap scripts with a partner and edit each other's work to make it as powerful as you can. Practise presenting the link before recording it yourself and discussing the results with a group.

Radio audiences

Radio is no different from any other media form when it comes to thinking about audiences. It needs to know clearly who it is talking to.

Every station wants to get as many people to listen to their output as they possibly can. The BBC Radio stations – local and national – have to prove that enough people listen to them to justify their public funding. Commercial radio stations only exist if they can persuade businesses to buy time to advertise. If no one is listening, advertisers will take their money to a station with big audiences.

So radio stations need listeners, but they cannot all have the same types of listeners. What your mum or dad likes is probably a bit different from what you like – whether clothes, music, food or radio programmes. For a radio station, defining its **target audience** is very important.

Take, for example, Gemini FM, which broadcasts to an area of Devon that includes Exeter, Torquay and a lot of small rural towns and villages. This is what they think about their niche audience:

> To talk about a 'typical listener' it is easier to refer to a single example. In terms of Gemini FM this is a twenty-five-year-old female who lives in the mainstream of British popular culture, loves eating and drinking and holidays abroad. She is permanently based in the local area and always enjoys a good night out on the town. She loves to spend money – mainly on clothes and fashion, music, magazines, DVDs and other products she's probably seen advertised. This woman is more likely to be a family-driven individual, maybe with young children, and deals with the pressure this brings. She has a passion for television and particularly loves the soaps, celebrity gossip, *This Morning* and *Big Brother*.
>
> It is important to note that Gemini FM is not a female brand. Nothing at the station should alienate our male audience. So why do we specifically target females? Extensive research has proved that men will willingly listen to a station directed at women but it will not work the other way round. In most cases, women tend to be 'rulers' of the household and it is often their choice of station to which the household radio will be tuned! So, by targeting women, we automatically attract the husbands and kids.

So Gemini will use this as a broad guide for what they will call their **audience profile**. But of course it is not as simple as that. They know that at different times of the day there will potentially be different sorts of audience profile. And so they divide their output up into a *clock* to match the things their audience are doing.

The Breakfast slot is an important start to the day, and a station's programming will reflect the fact that all the family are getting ready for work or school. So *survival information* – traffic reports, weather, regular time checks – is a prominent part of the programme content. By mid-morning, listeners will be at work or back home. In Gemini's case, thinking of a typical listener who is 25 and female will guide the type of presenter chosen and the content for that show. The early evening show tends to attract a younger listener, so the musical content and presenter's style will reflect this.

7 Gemini FM presenters

This broad outline of the types of programme played round the clock is called a *programme schedule*. Deciding on the programme schedule for the station is the responsibility of the *programme controller*.

Is there anybody out there?

Even though radio stations have a clear idea about the types of people they think are listening, they need constantly to check on their **audience share**. They do this by using the information provided by a company called RAJAR (Radio Joint Audience Research).

Station	Survey period	Adults 15+ in 000s	Weekly reach		Average hours of listening		Total hours in 000s	Share of potential listeners as %
			in 000s	%	Head	Listener		
BBC Radio Northampton	H	432	86	20.0	3.4	17.0	1454	12.9

8 Specimen data from the RAJAR website

The sample of data from RAJAR in **8** shows the audience data for just one radio station. The same information is provided for every radio station in the country. Use these notes to help you understand the table.

Survey period: based on figures from a Quarter (Q), Half (H) or Full (F) Year.

Adults 15+ in 000s: the total number of adults over 15 who live in the broadcast area for this station. BBC Radio Northampton broadcasts to an area with 432 000 adults over 15 in its reach.

Weekly reach in 000s: the number of people (in thousands) who listened to the station in the sample period. For BBC Northampton this was 86 000.

Weekly reach %: percentage of the total population of the area who listened to the station in the sample period. For BBC Northampton this was 20 per cent.

Average hours of listening Head: total time spent listening by the head of the household.

Average hours of listening Listener: total number of hours for all people in the household.

Total hours in 000s: total amount of time that people in the area listened to this station. For BBC Northampton this was 1 454 000 hours.

Share of listening as %: This very important figure tells each station how big a share of the market they have managed to attract to their station. For BBC Northampton this was 12.9 per cent during this sample period.

> ### ACTIVITY 5
>
> Visit the RAJAR website via www.heinemann.co.uk/hotlinks. Look up your own local radio stations, both independent and BBC. Which do you think is the most successful station?

How do RAJAR find these figures?

Like all statistics of this sort, RAJAR's data is based on the response from a sample of listeners. RAJAR Limited was established in 1992 to operate a single audience measurement system for the radio industry. Results are published quarterly by monitoring a sample selection from every radio station's TSA (Total Survey Area).

- Listening diaries are distributed by RAJAR into selected households in each area of the country. They have to be completed within seven days.
- Diaries are placed with one selected adult over the age of 15 and up to two others in each household.
- The diary's pages are broken down into fifteen-minute intervals each day. The family fill in which radio station they listened to and for how long.
- Every radio station in the family's broadcast area is included in the diary.
- The diaries are collected by RAJAR at the end of the seven-day period. The data are collated and distributed to participating radio stations and to the public via the RAJAR website.

Radio news

Most radio stations will broadcast news bulletins at some points during the day. The national BBC station, 5 Live, was set up to provide listeners mainly with news and sports coverage all day. Local commercial radio stations will usually broadcast short news summaries once an hour. So whoever you are, the radio station bosses think that you will want to hear a bit of news.

In an age with 24-hour rolling TV news, it is easy to imagine that all news journalists rush around the globe, chasing action-packed stories about war, crime or other high-profile events. While this may be true for a few of the top reporters, most radio newsrooms around the country will spend their whole time on their local patch. The sources of their news are not secret meetings with dangerous war lords, but are much more mundane. Most news on local radio will come from one of these sources (look back at pages 77–78 for more details):

- Agendas for council meetings
- Press releases
- Police voice bank
- Fire and Rescue services fax back

- News Agencies

- Contacts

- National stories from Independent Radio News

- Members of the public phoning the station with news of incidents or events

- Newspapers/Teletext/TV/Sky: radio journalists will double check these sources to see if they have any local stories they might be missing

- Journalists using their eyes and ears: chat in the pub, a big poster opposing a new supermarket development, fire engines heading into town, etc.

ACTIVITY 6

Listen to one news broadcast on your local radio station. Which of the above sources do you think might have provided the content for each item reported?

How are news items chosen?

The station's view of its audience determines which news items they include and where they are placed in the bulletin's running order. If the audience is largely made up of thirty-something parents who own their own home and juggle work with family life, news journalists will assume they will be interested in stories to do with house prices, health, education as well as what is happening in their town/village/city.

Another factor affecting what gets in and what gets left out – especially where it is a local radio station's news bulletin – is the distinction between *need-to-know* stories and *want-to-know* stories. Need-to-know items are stories that you would hear if you tuned into another local station or TV news bulletin; they are the main stories of the day. Want-to-know items are stories that local journalists have discovered using their own sources and think their audience will want to know about.

ACTIVITY 7 EXTENSION

1 Record one minute of a news bulletin from each of the following radio stations:
   - BBC Radio 5 Live
   - BBC Radio 1
   - Your local commercial radio station.

2 Play the recordings back and copy down exactly the words of each of the news bulletins. This will produce what is called a *transcript* of the news.

3 With a partner, compare the three transcripts. What do the type of language and the content of the news tell us about the target audience for each station?

Key area	What you have learned
Media language	• That music, speech and sound effects are the common features of any radio station. • That the ways in which each of those three components is used will give a distinctive *house style*.
Audiences	• That different radio stations target different audiences. • Knowing exactly who is listening to a station is essential information for the programme controllers of radio stations. • Very detailed information is provided to radio stations about their audience share.
Institutions and organisations	• Independent commercial radio stations only exist if they can attract enough advertisers – because advertisers pay the bills. • The BBC is funded from the Licence fee and is able to run stations which might otherwise not exist.
Representation	• The events and ideas reported in radio news will be affected by the sources who provide the information on which the news reports are based.

In this unit you will find out:

- how magazine advertisements use written and gesture codes to convey meaning
- how advertisers on TV and radio categorise, measure and target their audiences
- how magazines and commercial TV and radio depend on their advertisers for funding
- how advertisements represent social groups and the past in stereotypically attractive ways.

TALKING POINT

Think of the three advertisements that you have enjoyed most on TV recently. Share your ideas with the class. Talk about:

- why you like them
- what sorts of products they advertised
- whether they persuaded you to buy the products.

TV advertising

Many of the advertisements you picked out will be for the sorts of products that you buy – or hope to buy one day! Obviously you have seen the ads, so you must have been watching TV when they were on. Advertisements on TV are very expensive, so advertisers make sure that they are shown when the people who might buy their product are viewing – different adverts are shown at different times of day.

ACTIVITY 1

1 Your advertising agency has been asked to organise TV slots for the four groups of advertisements **A–D** shown in **1** opposite. The table below shows the slots that are available. Decide when to show each group of adverts.

	1	2	3	4
Programme	*Countdown*	*European Football Champions League*	*Globe Trekker*	*Pop Favourites*
Channel	4	ITV 1	Discovery Channel	MTV2
Days	Weekdays	Tuesdays/ Wednesdays	Daily	Daily
Time	3.15pm	7.30pm	Afternoons	5pm

2 Talk about your choices. How did you make your decisions?

KEY TERMS

Category group of consumers or viewers that share certain characteristics, such as age or income

Impact when a viewer watches the programme; impacts are counted to show how many viewers a programme has

Stereotyping assuming that a group of people all behave similarly

Universe the maximum number of viewers in a category that might watch a programme

A

British Airways long-haul flights

Johnsons baby wipes

Tesco supermarket

B

Adidas sportswear

Lucozade soft drink

Nikon digital camera

C

Fixiadent denture fixative

Saga holidays for over 50s

Stannah stairlift

D

American Express credit card

Ford high-performance car

Wilkinson Sword razor

1 Choose suitable slots for these groups of advertisements

As you found in Activity 1, advertising on television is targeted at specific age and interest groups – the *target audience*. Viewers are divided into **categories** – the number of people in a category that could be watching is called a **universe**. Placing an advertisement with programmes or times that attract them can target the desired groups. For example, children can be targeted by using slots on Children's Independent Television (CITV), and a broad group of adults by slots in peak viewing like *Coronation Street*. Every time a viewer in a particular category watches a TV programme it counts as an **impact** for that category of viewer. More often than not an advertiser is targeting more than one category.

Advertisers target people based on **stereotyping**. They assume, for example, not only that all 20–30-year-old males watch football, but that they all drink beer and want fast cars. Although this is clearly not true, it is true often enough for the targeting to work. You can see the categories in the ACORN system, used widely by advertisers, in **2**.

ACORN category	ACORN group	Percentage of population, 2002
A – Thriving		
1	Wealthy achievers, suburban areas	15.0
2	Affluent greys, rural communities	2.1
3	Prosperous pensioners, retirement areas	2.6
B – Expanding		
4	Affluent executives, family areas	4.1
5	Well-off workers, family areas	8.0
C – Rising		
6	Affluent urbanites, town and city areas	2.5
7	Prosperous professionals, metropolitan areas	2.3
8	Better-off executives, inner-city areas	3.8
D – Settling		
9	Comfortable middle-agers, mature homeowning areas	13.6
10	Skilled workers, homeowning areas	10.7
E – Aspiring		
11	New homeowners, mature communities	9.6
12	White-collar workers, better-off multiethnic areas	4.0
F – Striving		
13	Older people, less prosperous areas	3.6
14	Council estate residents, better-off homes	10.8
15	Council estate residents, high unemployment	2.8
16	Council estate residents, greatest hardship	2.3
17	People in multiethnic, low-income areas	2.0

2 An example of the categories used by advertisers

Ratings

For companies trying to sell their products, television **ratings** are very important because they show what percentage of the potential audience actually viewed the programme. Ratings are measured in TVRs: 1 TVR is 1 per cent of the potential audience. On Boxing Day 2003, 6.5 million people watched *The Office*, out of a universe of 21.6 million, giving a rating of 30 per cent, or 30 TVRs.

Ratings are calculated from viewing figures produced by the Broadcasters' Audience Research Board (BARB). Panels of television-owning households are monitored, representing the viewing behaviour of over 24 million households in the UK. Television and video viewing in the panel households is monitored electronically. Data are available for any channel at any minute of the day.

Advertisers are not going to spend a fortune promoting their products during a show that has poor ratings. The higher the ratings, the more the advertising slot costs. Each minute of a break has a value and cost per thousand viewers.

KEY TERM

Ratings the number of people who watch the programme as calculated by BARB (Broadcasters' Audience Research Board)

Strategies used to sell products

You have looked at where companies place their television adverts to make the maximum impact. How do adverts work to attract the audience to the products?

In the 1970s Abraham Maslow suggested that human behaviour is focused on satisfying certain basic types of needs. Adverts are designed to show you how buying or using a product can help you satisfy these needs. They may address needs directly, saying: 'I'll bet you're hungry! Have one of these chocolate bars!' Or they may be less obvious, making you identify with the situation in the advert and see yourself in it. Most adverts appeal to a combination of needs.

How advertisements use human needs

- **Need to survive**   Used by advertisements for food, drink, housing, etc.

- **Need to feel safe**   Advertisements for insurance, loans and banks promise security and freedom from threats.

- **Need for affiliation or friendship**   Adverts that focus on lifestyle choices like diet and fashion use people's desire to be popular. They may also threaten them with the failure to be liked or fit in.

- **Need to nurture or care for something**   Advertising which shows cute animals and small children brings this out in the viewer.

- **Need to achieve**   Advertisements that are linked with winning, often promoted by sports personalities, tap into the need to succeed at difficult tasks.

- **Need for attention**   Advertisements for beauty products often play on the need to be noticed and admired.

- **Need for prominence**   Advertisements for expensive furniture and diamonds may use people's need to be respected and to have high social status.

- **Need to dominate**   Advertisements for products like fast cars offer the possibility of being in control through the product.

- **Need to find meaning in life**   Advertisements for travel or music may appeal to people's need for fulfilment.

ACTIVITY 2

1   Think of a TV advert which plays on each of the needs above. Explain how it does so.

2   Try to think of other needs used to promote products that are not mentioned here.

Case study: the Bertolli campaign

A feature of television advertising is the long-running campaign with a particular theme or slogan. The TV adverts for Bertolli are a good example of this. The Mediterranean diet of fruit, fish and vegetables has been shown to encourage a long and healthy life. Bertolli uses this idea to advertise its products: a range of spreads, olive oils and pasta sauces.

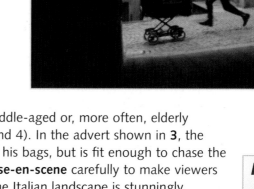

3 Bertolli ads show elderly people as healthy and active – and cunning

The characters in the commercials are usually middle-aged or, more often, elderly people who are enjoying fun-filled lives (see **3** and 4). In the advert shown in **3**, the elderly man allows the pretty young girl to carry his bags, but is fit enough to chase the pram down the hill. The director chooses the **mise-en-scene** carefully to make viewers desire this lifestyle: the sun always shines, and the Italian landscape is stunningly beautiful. The message is that eating Bertolli products will help you to live a long time – and that there is plenty to look forward to!

The advert offers a **representation** of life in Tuscany as being without the stresses of everyday life. In reality Tuscan winters can be cold, and summer work in the olive groves long and physically demanding.

As well as being healthy, the characters have romance in their lives. In one advert, the village has a new doctor, a very handsome young man. The old ladies paint spots on their faces to have an excuse to go and see him. This contradicts the usual **stereotype** of elderly women by showing them as still interested in good-looking young men. What message does this convey to female viewers? Remember, it is usually women that decide which brand of oil or spread to buy.

4 Healthy eating is shown as leading to a long and active life – notice the spread on the table

ACTIVITY 3

Try to watch another advert for Bertolli or one for another product that is set overseas.

1   What message does it convey? How does it use mise-en-scene, stereotyping and humour to convey this message?

2   Which human needs does it address?

Intertextuality

Intertextuality is another important strategy used in advertising. Some media texts create part of their meaning by referring to other media texts that the makers assume most of the audience will know. The advert must work for those who do not know the reference, but for those who get the point, there is a 'feel good' factor that transfers itself to the product.

Intertextual references are used in the Bertolli campaign to reinforce the theme of 'eternal youth':

●   Some Bertolli adverts use the slogan 'Club 18–130', making an intertextual reference to the young people's holiday packages 'Club 18–30'.

●   An advert for a new spread used the theme of the *Romeo and Juliet* story – even using some lines from this Shakespeare play. The big difference was that the lovers were in their eighties and the story had a happy ending!

Intertextuality is used in more complex ways in a Bertolli advert entitled *The Olive Oil Barons of Italy*:

●   The advert copies the visual style of the title sequence of *Dallas*, a very popular 1970s TV series about a Texan family who had made a fortune from oil.

●   The advert uses the *Dallas* signature tune, but played on a mandolin, suggesting an Italian setting.

●   'Bertolli family members' are shown in poses associated with *Dallas*, but they are either elderly or stereotypically glamorous young Italians.

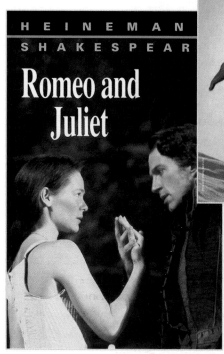

5 Bertolli have used intertextual references to *Romeo and Juliet*, Club 18–30 and *Dallas* in their campaigns

Changing styles of advertising campaigns

Fashions change in advertising as well as in clothing. You can follow these changes by looking at advertisements for Hovis®, a brand established in 1886.

In the 1920s advertisements were targeted at mothers and children, showing the bread's nutritional benefits for children. However, in the next decade, as touring by car became more and more popular, motorists were targeted by signs on cafés all over the country saying 'Teas with Hovis'.

6 This Hovis advertisement appeared in the 1950s

The slogan 'Don't say Brown – say Hovis', first used in 1916, was used in the brand's early TV commercials in the 1950s, featuring a famous comedian of the time. Print-based advertisements also used the slogan (**6**). Adverts such as **6** showed a particular idealised view of family life – after the hardships of wartime, plentiful food and healthy, happy families were symbols of an exciting and prosperous post-war Britain.

7 *Bike Ride* (1974)

By the late 1960s, however, people were disillusioned with change and the 'new' and looked back nostalgically at life before the war. Hovis adverts reflected this by using a very different approach. Their campaign in the 1970s and 1980s took as its central theme the idea that Hovis bread had been around a long time and had not changed. The slogan now was 'As good today as it's always been'.

The central characters were young boys shown in the dress and settings of the early 1900s. *Bike Ride* (1974) was directed by Ridley Scott, later famous for films such as *Gladiator*, and won many awards (see **7**). It shows a boy delivering loaves of bread on cobbled streets; he is seen pushing his bike up a steep hill, making his delivery then freewheeling at speed down the hill again. The voice-over is the boy as an old man, remembering with pleasure the events shown in the advert.

The advert plays on feelings of nostalgia – a view of the past as the good old days when life was uncomplicated and generally happy. By being associated with this positive feeling, the product takes on an image of being something good and wholesome that has survived from the past. The slogan reinforces this idea. It appeals to people's needs to be safe and to be affiliated with earlier generations.

However, was the past really like this? Life in a mill town in the early 1900s was very different from the one the adverts portray. The representation leaves out the hardships of life, such as long working hours for little money and few material possessions. It focuses instead on community spirit and simple pleasures. The past is seen as a place of safety and good honest fun, filtering out the less pleasant realities.

TIP

You can find out more about the Hovis campaigns. Use the Heinemann Hotlinks site to visit the Hovis website.

ACTIVITY 5

1   Discuss in pairs the appeal to an audience of an advert that uses nostalgia to sell a product.
2   Imagine you are producing an advert in 50 years' time to relaunch either a brand of crisps or 'retro' football boots. Choose images from our times that will arouse feelings of nostalgia in the audience. Storyboard a short narrative sequence that presents our present lives as happy and carefree.

Even the most successful companies have to change the image of their products from time to time to attract the attention of the audience. To do this successfully, they need to gauge the mood of the audience and relate to their needs and concerns. By 2003 Hovis had abandoned nostalgia and looked instead at what life is really like for most of us (see **8**).

8 The family in the Hovis advertisement for Best of Both, 2003

The advert for Hovis Best of Both – soft white bread with wheatgerm – features an animated scene where brother and sister squabble about everything except bread! It shows that, while family life is far from perfect, the product offers something that unites them. The advert is aimed at the children's mother: what good feelings about the product will she take from this text? Will these be very different from the feelings of the mother targeted by the advert in **6**?

ACTIVITY 6 EXTENSION

1 Examine the ways in which companies such as Levi Strauss Jeans and Lucozade have changed the images of their products over time. You can access their websites using a search engine. Write about:
- the new image of the product
- the strategies used to advertise it.

2 Design an advertising campaign for a product that needs a change of image, such as thermal underwear or prunes.
- Decide on the audience you will target, and which needs you will address.
- Think of a new name and a slogan for your product.
- Storyboard a television advert or design a poster to advertise your product.

Regulation of advertising

Makers of television adverts find many inventive ways to get their messages across in a matter of seconds. However, there are limits to what they can do. TV advertising is monitored by the Independent Television Commission (ITC) and must be 'legal, decent, honest and truthful'. This means that they may not, for example:

- use bad or blasphemous language

- show an advert that is unsuitable for children before the 9pm watershed

- represent women in a sexist way

- use violent or sexually explicit material

- give false facts about their own or rival products.

Advertising of all types is regulated by the Advertising Standards Authority (ASA), which was set up in 1962. The Advertising Code gives the principles that all makers of advertisements, in any media form, should follow in matters of taste and decency.

The Code has specific guidelines about the advertising of alcoholic drink. Drinking alcohol must not be represented as daring or clever, or as bringing success in relationships or other areas of life. It must also be obvious that the people appearing in the advert are old enough to drink legally.

In 2001 the ASA investigated 4312 complaints, of which 2439 were upheld. The advert receiving the most complaints (211) was a mailshot for slimming pills that appeared to be a recommendation from a friend. These complaints were upheld.

Radio advertising

Every radio station carries some form of advertising. BBC stations advertise BBC radio and TV programmes and websites. For commercial radio, advertising is all-important – it pays for the entire running costs of each station.

Running a radio station is an expensive business. Money must be found for:

● rent, heating, lighting and phone bills

● salaries and training for presenters, writers, technical and administrative staff and the sales team

● promoting the station: mugs, car stickers, local advertising, promotional vehicles

● buying the Licence which allows commercial radio to broadcast locally

● paying the royalty fees incurred every time a piece of music is played

● the latest technology

● competition prizes.

Commercial radio stations are public limited companies (plc). They must make a profit to pay to their shareholders each year.

How much does radio advertising cost?

The cost of an advert or *spot* on commercial radio varies enormously according to a number of factors:

● **The length of the advert** can be from 10 to 60 seconds: the longer the spot, the higher the cost.

● **When the advert is broadcast:** the radio industry regulator allows approximately 10 minutes per hour for advertisements. Once the airtime has been sold no more spots can be created. When there is high demand for airtime, then spots are more expensive.

● **The popularity of the station:** radio stations with more listeners can charge more for their spots – national networks can usually charge more than local ones.

● **Time of day:** adverts shown between 6am and 7pm cost more than those going out overnight because there are more listeners then. For the same reason, adverts are more expensive during the flagship Breakfast Show than during the Drivetime Show.

● **Day of the week:** an advert at the end of the week costs more because large national retailers buy advertising space on Thursdays and Fridays in bulk, to influence listeners before they do their weekend shopping.

● **Time of the year:** spots cost more just before Christmas, Easter and other holidays, when demand is high.

● **Length of campaign:** radio stations often charge regular advertisers who advertise all year less per spot than clients who run a short-term campaign, for example to publicise their January Sales.

> **TIP**
>
> You could try to find out what the actual rates are by phoning your local station and asking them to send you a *rate card*.

How magazine and newspaper adverts create desires

As you know, advertising works by satisfying the consumer's needs (page 155). However, these needs are not always apparent to the consumer until the advertisement has created a desire. One way this is done is by offering you, the future buyer, an image of yourself made to look more glamorous, powerful or popular as a result of using the product. This image is designed to make you envious of the way you might be and see yourself transformed by the product into the envy of others, an envy which will give you permission to love yourself enough to spend the money.

Magazines and newspaper pages for women in particular feature advertisements of this type. The readers rarely *need* in any real sense the fashion and beauty products that they promote – a need must be created. How is desire created by the perfume advert in **9**. What image is suggested by the model and the way she is presented? Can you think of other ways the advert works that are not given on the image?

Targeting an audience

Adverts can be targeted at a very specific audience. Adverts in some magazines target their audience by appearing in the magazine that they read. Choosing the correct magazine is not that simple, however. The object of desire offers the future buyer an image of themselves as they would like to be. Pre-teen girls would like to be older, so they buy magazines which feature older teenagers.

How do you open up a new market for your products and persuade a possibly hostile future buyer to want your product? In the advert in **10**, the challenge is to make men buy products normally bought by women. Some men may reject the idea because they see it as threatening their masculine self-image. How has the advert been constructed to address that concern? How many references to masculinity can you see in the advert?

The reader cannot see the top of the model's head; the camera is angled to look up at her, making her more imposing.

The model's hair is over one eye – a protest against a neat, ordered look? Perhaps defiance? Young people often rebel.

Her eyebrow is arched – is she questioning the onlooker? 'What are you looking at me for, what do you want?'

Her look is slightly boyish – which perfume does she wear? Both, depending on mood? It is fashionable for girls to wear men's fragrances.

Her skin is totally without blemish.

The background colour is warm peach blending into paler cream – peaches and cream complexion?

The product is displayed in sharp focus – easily recognisable in the shop.

Several font styles, both classic and modern, are used in the word *Bazar* – is the perfume both classic and modern?

Christain Lacroix is a famous designer – some people think his style is 'bizarre'.

The font used for the name has a hand-painted look, making the product seem exclusive.

French is used – French perfumes and clothes are seen as stylish, and French women are stereotypically modern and chic.

The bottle tops are futuristic in design – the perfume is new and modern.

9 Advertisement for the perfume Bazar by Christian Lacroix

10 This advert creates a desire for male grooming products

11 Who does this advertisement target?

Multimedia campaigns

You have seen how advertisers use television, radio, newspapers and magazines to promote their products. In practice, an advertising campaign will often involve more than one of these, and some other strategies as well.

There are several marketing tools that can be used individually or in combination:

- An airtime campaign on TV and/or radio
- Advertisements in the print media – newspapers and magazines
- Sponsorship
- Promotions
- The Internet
- Posters
- Mail drops.

Sponsorship

What do you think of when you hear the word 'sponsorship'? Sport, probably – but why do companies sponsor sports events and personalities? The answer is: to get their names seen and heard in the media, so that the public are constantly reminded of them.

An advertising message tends to be a 'selling message', while a sponsorship message is often a 'telling message'. *Coronation Street* is sponsored by a well known make of chocolate; the name of the chocolate is said, but there is no 'selling message' explaining why you should buy it.

On commercial radio the traffic feature, giving details of traffic problems in the area, is often sponsored by a motor dealership. This works well for the client because:

- they appear to be an integral part of the show, gaining from a transfer of **brand values** from the station
- the show targets car drivers at a time when they are a **captive audience**.

The better the match of client to the feature, the more credibility the client and station will have.

Sponsorship is often part of a multimedia campaign – a star footballer may wear a company's logo when he plays, appear in their TV adverts and take part in promotions. All this exposure can make the footballer an even greater star, increasing his value to the sponsor.

> **KEY TERMS**
>
> **Brand values** the type of lifestyle and image which the advertiser would like clients to associate with their product
>
> **Captive audience** a media audience who find it difficult not to consume the text, e.g. because they are driving a car
>
> **Sponsorship** the association of a client's name with a programme or product

Promotions

Occasionally a client may just want to promote immediate awareness of a one-off event, such as a store-opening by a celebrity. A series of advertisements will appear in the local media, and newspaper, TV and radio reporters will be invited to the opening. The local radio station may have a presenter at the store opening, giving away promotional products, and perhaps doing a small number of 'talk ups' on the radio, encouraging listeners to come to the store.

Promotional campaigns can stand alone or be a part of a wider marketing strategy. The cost of the campaign will depend on which strategies are chosen and for how long they are used.

The Internet

Most companies, large and small, have a website, and this can now be an important part of the marketing mix. Maintaining the site itself is relatively cheap, but means have to be found to direct potential customers to it.

An entry on a radio station's website is an added benefit to clients. Anyone who advertises for more than a minimum number of weeks will be able to appear free on the 'as advertised' section on the station website.

Other forms of advertising

Advertisers use poster campaigns on billboards and buses as relatively low-cost ways of promoting their products or services. Organisers of local events can put up word-processed posters in shop windows, often for nothing.

Mailshots and flyers included in newspapers are also used for both local and national campaigns. These can be targeted by postcode or sent to most households in the country, as is the case with some national charities.

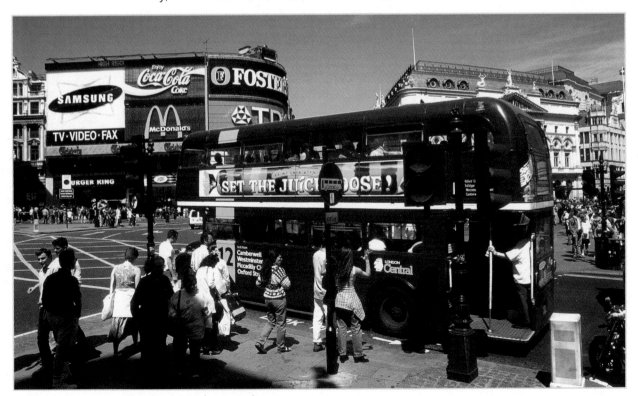

12 Advertising takes many forms

Another way that companies can make consumers familiar with their products is by *product placement*: consumer goods and foods are used conspicuously in TV programmes and films, creating a desire in the audience, especially one that wants to identify with the stars.

Designing a multimedia campaign

How does an advertising agency decide which components to use in a campaign? The two main factors are cost and target audience. Just like radio advertisements, the cost of TV and newspaper and magazine adverts varies according to length or size, timing and the size of the potential audience.

ACTIVITY 10

In pairs, decide which forms of advertising you would use in a campaign for:

- the high-budget national launch of a new brand of chewing gum
- a school fundraising event featuring a local celebrity
- a cable TV company moving into a new area.

UNIT SUMMARY

Key area	What you have learned
Media language	• How adverts communicate meaning • How adverts use intertextuality and subvert stereotypes
Audiences	• How future buyers read adverts • How advertisers target TV, radio and magazine audiences
Institutions and organisations	• How advertising reflects changing times • How advertising is controlled • How magazines and commercial TV and radio depend on advertisers for funding
Representation	• How adverts represent different social groups: the elderly, young women, young men • How adverts represent places • How adverts represent the past

9 Succeeding with practical media production work

In this unit you will find out:

- how to use media technologies to produce a high-quality product
- how to shape your product to suit its audience
- how to follow the same stages as professionals in producing your work
- how to choose the ways in which you represent ideas, issues and people.

Production work is a very interesting part of your GCSE Media Studies course because this is when you get to use cameras or computer software to produce something of your choice. This also counts for a substantial proportion of the marks, so it will not only satisfy your creativity but can gain you useful marks.

Learning on the job

As well as providing an enjoyable opportunity to get behind a video camera or make your own magazine, production tasks should help you to learn more about the way the media work. You may have written about films, radio programmes or magazines during your course. Making a version of one of these for yourself should show you useful things about the way these media texts are put together.

Whatever type of production work you choose, there are three key words you need to remember: planning, planning and planning! Without a clear plan of attack you will soon get frustrated and your work will not do you justice. This unit will help you to get the most from practical work by making you think like a professional.

When you plan your work, think of the three stages used by the media industry:

- **Pre-production** – progress towards a finished production, including research and planning

- **Production** – using technology to collect the material you need to get your film, magazine or radio programme made

- **Post-production** – assembling all the photos, recordings and interviews into a finished product.

There will, of course, be a few differences between your practical production and a Steven Spielberg movie. Although you will do your best to make it look like the real thing, your school may not have all the very latest equipment. Examiners do not expect you to match the professionals who have a lot more time, money and equipment than you do. The point of this part of the course is to give you experience of some of the processes used by the media so that you can understand them better, and also to develop your creativity.

Group or solo?

Professional films, magazines, radio programmes and display advertisements are always team efforts. In the case of a feature film, many hundreds of people will have worked on the production.

You need to decide whether to do your Practical Production as part of a group of up to four or on your own. For some types of practical production, such as video-making, it is virtually impossible to work alone. For the other types, group work can be helpful: two or three views and sets of ideas are likely to make for a more interesting final product. You can find more details about working in a group in the introduction.

Writing an analysis and evaluation of your work

Another difference between your GCSE production and professionally produced material is that once the editor of *Smash Hits* has published the magazine, they do not have to write an account of how good they think it is. But you do!

The analysis and evaluation (also known as a *supporting account, written evaluative report* or *evaluative commentary*) form a very important part of the work you will do and of your marks (see the example on page 191). If you are working in a group, it is doubly important because it will show the individual contribution you made towards the work (see pages 10–11).

The written evaluation should fall within the word count limits given by your awarding body (see pages 10–11). It should include:

- A clear opening explanation of what you were intending to produce and the target audience at whom you aimed your production.

- Some evidence that you have thought about, and preferably researched, your target audience and the 'market' for your product.

- Your own comments on the decisions that were made at each stage of production and why those decisions were made. For example, if you had three video sequences of a particular section of your film and only chose one to include in the final edit – *why* were the other two rejected? These comments on the decision-making process will be very important for your teacher when the marks are being given because it shows how much you have learnt from doing the production work.

- In a group production, a clear account of all the things you were responsible for.

- Links between your product and professionally produced work of a similar nature. How and why is yours different?

- A final evaluation of the completed production, saying how successful you think it is, what you would change if you had the chance to do it again and a statement about what you have learnt as a result of the work.

- An appendix to your written piece which includes pre-production work such as storyboards, questionnaires, scripts and work schedules.

You should *not* include:

- A string of excuses about your teacher failing to give you the right camera/computer/battery.

- A minute-by-minute account of every button that was pushed and tripod that was carried – what examiners call the 'dear Diary' approach. You only have a limited number of words, not enough to waste describing unimportant details.

Research

An important part of pre-production is the research stage. Before you rush headlong into designing your advertising campaign or shooting your pop video, you will need to think about the content of your product and the audience you are aiming it at.

Any company launching a new teen magazine in the real world would first find out about the interests and needs of the teenagers they hope to persuade to buy their magazine. They would also analyse very carefully their target audience and the products already in the market.

For some types of product you may find it useful to do some market research. This need not necessarily take the form of detailed questionnaires – though that is a possibility. But you should at the very least try out any ideas you have on some representative sample of your target audience to gauge their reaction. You should then write up what you have learnt from the research in your analysis.

Another part of your research will probably have been covered during your GCSE Media Studies course. This is a study of the way in which media texts like yours are put together. In other words, you should be familiar with the *media language* you are about to use. An important part of producing a good practical production is the extent to which you have shown your teacher and the examiner that you understand and can use effectively the *codes* and *conventions* of your chosen medium.

What does this mean in practice? Suppose you are producing a radio magazine programme aimed at a teenage market about the latest film releases. If all you do is sit down in front of a tape recorder and talk in a monotone about a few films you have seen recently, you will not have used appropriate media language. A professional programme of this sort would include interviews, extracts of dialogue from some films, and a synopsis of what the films are about and who appears in them. The presentation would be slick, with no long pauses or 'ums' and 'errs'. Usually some sort of outline script guides the way the programme develops.

Choosing your medium

With your research completed, you now need to decide which type or types of media technology you are going to use to complete your production work. Ideally you will have tried your hand at a variety of print, audio and video projects during your course so you will know your own expertise and preferences. If not, it is important as part of pre-production to practise with the type of equipment you are going to use. If you start trying to shoot a video or record a radio programme for the first time during the production phase you are less likely to do yourself full justice.

Making a video

Video is arguably the most exciting technology to use for your practical work. It is really a multi-technology because you will be dealing with pictures, sounds and maybe graphic designs too.

For these reasons it is also the most complex. To get the best results you must be sure to plan every stage in the greatest possible detail. Because there are a number of different stages and activities involved in making a video production, it is a good choice for a group. Everyone will certainly have enough chance to make their own individual contribution.

One thing you should be clear about right from the outset: small is beautiful. A thirty-second advertisement can involve a tremendous amount of hard work and planning. It is better to think in terms of a short but highly crafted video than a ten- or fifteen-minute epic. The longer the video, the less attention is paid to getting each shot as tightly composed and appropriately edited as it ought to be.

Pre-production

Storyboarding your ideas

Designing and drawing the storyboard form a vital part of the pre-production phase. A storyboard is the visual part of a film set down on paper or computer screen to look like a strip of pictures from a comic. Alongside the pictures or drawings are notes which give details of any dialogue to be spoken, any music soundtrack or sound effects, camera movements like pans or tracks, movements made by actors and sometimes notes about costume, props and, if appropriate, lighting.

Why is a storyboard important?

● To get visual ideas out of your head and onto paper/screen: this is often the most difficult stage of the whole filming process. Storyboarding forces you to clarify your ideas and think carefully about how to get your meaning across to the audience through pictures.

● To plan the order of the shots in a sequence: think where the camera will be placed and what movements your actors will be making.

● To save time on location: if you arrive with no idea of how the film is to be shot you will be wasting everyone's time.

Storyboarding a film

If your school has a software package such as Storyboard you can use that to storyboard your film. However, a paper version of your storyboard will do just as well. Whatever version of a storyboard you use, it should contain columns with the information shown in chart **1**.

Visuals	Shot type	Words	Music/FX	Timing
You will need to draw into this box exactly what you want the camera operator to see and film. The drawing does not need to be beautifully finished, but it must show what it is that you want to happen during the filming of this particular shot.	This is a quick back-up to your drawing in the Visuals box. It will use the common abbreviations to indicate which shot types and camera angles you wish to be used. See pages 22–24 and 39 for details of shot types.	This box will contain any words of dialogue or voice-over that accompany the shot in the visuals box.	The music is likely to run beneath a number of shots, so this column may have an arrow continuing from the boxes above showing which shots it is covering – and noting precisely which shot it begins with and at which shot it ends. The same may be true for special effects, or there may be a short noise which only occurs in this shot.	In this column show the duration of the shot or sequence.

1 How to lay out a storyboard sheet for a film

2 This student's completed storyboard for a photo-comic could be adapted to make a short film

Production

The production stage involves making the ideas on your storyboard into shots taken by a camera crew. You not have to shoot everything in exactly the same order as it comes on your storyboard, especially if it involves different locations. You can put things into the right order in the edit at the post-production stage.

Shot log

To save you time when you come to edit, it is a good idea always to keep a **shot log** (see the example in **3**). If you are using a sophisticated camera, you might be able to record the time code on the logging sheet, to give you an exact reference in seconds for each shot on the tape.

If, as is more likely, you are working with simpler equipment, you need to log how long the shot is and a *cumulative time,* that is, how many minutes of tape have been shot in all. This will help you find them more quickly when you come to edit. In this case it is a good idea to use a *clapper board.* All you need is a small blackboard and chalk, or a white board and marker pen. Every time you roll the camera, focus first on the clapper board on which you have written the exact shot number and take number.

Camera operator: *JG*   Location: *Lydford*
Camera: *Canon XM 1*   Date: *4th June 04*

Shot no.	Set up: ELS/LS/ MLS/MS/MCU/ CU/ECU	Take Good (G) or No good (NG)?	Notes on shot content	Time code
1	*ELS*	*NG*	*Tripod knocked*	*00: 31: 14*
1	*ELS*	*G*	*Shot down over the valley, showing village*	*00: 31: 27*
2	*LS*	*G*	*Tilt down church spire to door*	*00: 31: 46*

3 Your shot log should look like this

Lighting

Too many students forget all about the lighting for a shot. If the lighting is wrong, the shot will look dead – or even worse, things like the expressions on people's faces will not be seen because they are underlit. Light is a vital part of film-making – which is why the chief camera operator is called a 'lighting cameraman'.

Not all of you will have access to lighting – although you should certainly try to get hold of some if you possibly can. If not, try to think of inventive ways to use candles, torches, car headlights – all of these can provide effective light sources. If you have no lighting of any sort then avoid filming in gloomy interiors, and think about the way you use natural light in exterior locations. Avoid standing your actor with the sun behind them unless you really want a silhouette effect.

Setting up lighting

It is helpful to think about three points where you can set up lights – two points in front of the action and one point behind it:

- **Key light:** This is the main light used on the set. It will be placed to one side of the camera and directed at the actors it is lighting.

- **Fill light:** This is placed on the other side of the camera from the Key light and is not as powerful. It takes out some, though not all, of the shadows created by the Key light.

- **Back light:** This is placed behind the figure. It defines the figure's outline and separates them from the background, giving a more three-dimensional effect to the shot.

You can also use what is called *practical lighting*. These are things which actually appear in shot, like a table lamp or a candle.

TIP

If you can access *MediaStage* software, use it to try out your lighting ideas. A print out of your screen shots could be used as evidence.

Planning your lighting

Lighting is used in film-making in two main ways:

- **Realistic lighting**: when successful, actors and set are lit so naturally and unobtrusively that the audience do not notice the technology that has been used to simulate reality. This approach is used, for example, in romantic comedies and soap operas.

- **Expressive lighting**: when the director uses light to set a mood or tone for a scene – or even a 'look' to a whole film. Films like *The Matrix* (1999) or *Moulin Rouge* (2001) have expressive lighting designs.

There are all sorts of variations that can be used when lighting shots. The best thing to do is try out different lighting set-ups until you get the one you think is best suited to the shot. However, it helps to think of two quite distinct types of lighting:

- **High-key picture:** This type of lighting makes the shot look very bright overall with small areas of shadow (see **4**); a bright sunlit outdoor shot would be high key.

- **Low-key picture:** The shot looks dark overall with few areas of highlight (see **5**). Night shots or interiors are often low-key. There may be one section of the shot which is quite brightly lit while the rest is in deep shadow.

When you are planning the lighting for any sequence in your film, use the prompt questions on page 176 to guide your decision-making. You should record the reasons for your decisions in your analysis.

4 High-key picture

5 Low-key picture

Style: Is the light to be high-key or low key? Or would you describe it in some other way?

Scene: Is the lighting being used to make the scene look like natural light or artificial light?

Angles: Is the placement of the key light from a high angle or a low angle?

Quality: Is the light going to give hard-edged shadows, as you would expect from very bright sunlight? Or will it create a softer, more diffuse look, as you would expect on a cloudy day?

Time: Is the shot to look as if it is early morning, midday, dusk or night-time?

Source: What is the source of the lighting in the scene intended to be? Remember – you can 'create' sunlight on a dull day by using strong artificial light to lift the light level.

Mood: This is probably the most important consideration. What mood or tone do you want to create? If you get the lighting wrong then the mood will be wrong and the shot will mean something different to the audience when they see your film.

6 Students setting up a shot

Sound

Much of the sound you hear on films has been added at the post-production stage, so you will look at sound again in that section. During production the **synchronised sound** is recorded.

The quality of the sound you record is as important as the quality of the picture, although it is far too often overlooked. Even if you only have the microphone which is mounted on your camera to work with, you can still plan to make sure you get the best sound possible. The golden rule is to get whatever microphone you are using as close to the person speaking as you possibly can.

Using an on-camera microphone
You will be limited by using this type of microphone because as well as the voice of the

Ambient sound the sounds of everything going on around the person who is speaking

Edit Decision List (EDL) or **Editing Script List** written statement of what is to go in the film and where it is to fit

Editor the person responsible for deciding the order in which shots and sequences are assembled at the post-production stage

Sequence a series of individual shots joined together by the editor

Synchronised sound the words spoken match the lip movements of the speaker

speaker you will pick up a lot of **ambient sound**. Sometimes you will want some ambient sound; if your actors are sitting on a beach you might want to hear the sound of waves and the wind. However, you need to control the level of those sounds so that they do not drown out the voice.

You will almost certainly need to set up shots that are no wider than a medium close-up, because the camera microphone will then be close enough to pick up a reasonable level of sound from the voice. If you are in a noisy environment, such as a busy street, you should move as close to the speaker as you reasonably can.

Using a microphone which is separate from the camera
The advantage of using an external microphone is that you can get it much closer to the person speaking while having the camera set at the type of shot you would ideally like – even if this is a long shot. Professional film crews have someone who does nothing else but record the sound. This sound recordist may use all sorts of different types of microphone, depending on the situation that is being filmed and the effect the director wants to achieve.

Post-production
The individual shots recorded during the production phase only make sense when they are joined together into **sequences**. It may help you to think of this as being like words building up into sentences. Each individual word may have some meaning. When you hear the word 'house' you have some picture in your mind of a building in which people live. But if words are added either side of it, the meaning is much clearer. 'The old house was falling down' gives you a much more detailed image to visualise. And of course if different words are put either side of 'house', the meaning is completely different: 'the glass house shimmered in the sun'. In exactly the same way, if you change the order in which your shots are combined into a sequence, the meaning can change.

Joining together the various shots into sequences is the job of the **editor**. Editing is a vitally important part of the whole film-making process. The director will very often work alongside the editor because the choices made at the editing stage can completely change the meaning of the finished piece.

Edit Decision List or Editing Script List
The first thing to do at post-production is to look at all the material you have shot and start to think about how it will all fit together. You cannot change the type of shot you or your group filmed, but for the edit you have to decide:

- how much of each shot is going to be included in the finished film
- the order in which the shots will be joined together into sequences.

When you have the basic building blocks in place, i.e. all the shots are in the right order and of the right length, then it is time to think of the finer details, such as transitions, visual effects and post-production sound.

Transitions
You get from one shot to the next by means of a *transition*. There are five main types.

- **The cut:** one shot is instantly followed on the screen by another. This is by far the most common transition. It is so common, in fact, that when it happens you hardly notice because you are so used to it.

All the other transitions are much more noticeable, so if you are thinking of using something other than a cut you should ask yourself: *What will that sort of transition add to my film that using a cut would not?*

TIP

If you can access *MediaStage* software, you can practise cuts and other editing techniques.

- **The jump cut:** the effect of a jump cut is to make the character on the screen appear to 'jump' from one place to another. It also makes the person watching jump because it disrupts the illusion that they are watching real life. A jump cut looks more like magic!

- **The dissolve:** the first shot gradually dissolves and is replaced by the second shot. There will be a moment when both shots are on the screen, before the first one gradually fades away.

- **The fade:** this can either be a *fade in*, which is where a blank screen is gradually filled by the incoming shot, or a *fade out* where the shot gradually fades away leaving a blank screen. The fade is usually used to show that, in the case of a fade in, a new scene is beginning, or with a fade out, that an ending of some sort has been reached.

- **The wipe:** the effect of a wipe is to see the first shot chased off the screen by the next shot. Wipes can use all sorts of different patterns to get one shot off and the next on. The incoming shot can burst through in the shape of a star or the outgoing shot can appear to swirl round and disappear like water running down a plug hole. Wipes will definitely draw attention to the fact that you are going from one shot to the next. Only use them if you have a *very* good reason.

Adding visual effects

Once again, unless there is a very good reason, avoid using too many visual effects. You should only use them when you have a clear idea of what effect you hope they will have on the viewer. Common visual effects you could use, if your editing software includes the option, include:

- desaturated colour: this gives a slightly washed out effect to the picture; you can even take out all the colour and make a black-and-white picture

- saturated colour: the colours are very vivid and unnatural

- slow motion

- fast motion.

Post-production sound

There are a few sound sources which you can think about adding to the synchronised sound you will already have recorded.

- **Voice-over sound**: this needs to be dubbed onto any picture sequences. Documentaries and advertisements often use a lot of voice-over.

- **Sound effects** will usually be added to the soundtrack at the dubbing stage. Sound effects can be further sub-divided into two types:
  - Those sounds which directly match actions or events on the screen, for example a door slamming or a glass breaking.

    – Those sounds which are about the scene but do not match anything actually shown. For example, the sound of birds singing might accompany a scene set in the countryside, or traffic noise and car horns dubbed onto a scene in a city centre flat. These sound effects are called *ambient sounds*. They appear on the soundtrack to give greater depth to the illusion that what is shown is real rather than something set up to be filmed.

● **Music** is the final sound to be added to your film in post-production. Your choice of music will be very important. Music is used to make the audience feel certain emotions as they watch the action on screen. In high-budget film or television productions, specially composed music will be commissioned for the soundtrack. Alternatively the rights to use well known pop songs can be bought.

The rough cut

With your EDL written, you are now ready to make a *rough cut* of your film. This is a bit like a first draft of a piece of writing. You need to implement all the decisions from the EDL and then sit back and view the rough cut a few times.

Until quite recently, editing was a very time-consuming business, mainly because any changes meant starting from the beginning and editing everything again. With new digital software packages that are cheap and easily available, editing can really become a drafting process.

7 Stages in the production of a video

It is not possible here to give detailed instructions about the process of using editing software because this will be different from one package to the next. If you are not familiar with the way the software works you will need to explore it before beginning your rough cut.

When viewing your rough cut, you need to think about these factors, and write about them in your analysis.

- **The length of time each shot is held on screen:** It is only when you see your rough cut that you will know whether your EDL got this right. If a shot contains one line spoken to camera by your actor then it cannot be shorter than the actual words being delivered. But is there a half-second pause that you could get rid of at the beginning to make the sequence flow more smoothly? Or does the shot end much too abruptly? Maybe an extra half second would make it less rushed? Remember – you can work as exactly as one twenty-fourth of a second so it pays to get the length of shot exactly right.

- **The order in which the shots occur:** Although you may have thought the order was correct when you were writing your EDL, on viewing them you may find that you can change them around, or even lose some altogether.

- **How well any visual effects, music or sound you have added work:** Does the music create the right mood for your film? Are the slow-motion sequences too slow or not slow enough? Do not be afraid to change things and see if they can be made to work more effectively – that is why you made a rough cut.

- **Have you got titles and end credits right?** Often you can leave the design of a title sequence until after you have viewed the rough. The same will be true for the end credits. But you will need to make sure everyone who has worked on or helped in the making of your film gets a mention.

The fine cut
Now that you have made all the notes on the changes to be made, you are ready to return to the editing software and make the final version – the fine cut – of your film.

Making a radio programme

In comparison to video-making, recording an audio product is potentially a much simpler process. It is possible to produce almost broadcast-quality results with relatively inexpensive equipment.

The type of recording gear you use will probably be dictated by the resources your school can provide. These days most radio stations use digital equipment, so interviews will be recorded on mini-disc players which slip into a journalist's coat pocket. But not long ago they were still recording on audio cassettes or open spool tape. Even if you only have access to audio-cassette machines, you can still make a radio programme which sounds pretty much like the real thing.

Pre-production
Once you have completed your research you will need to write a programme outline and then a running order of the items which are to appear. It is important to show that you can use a full range of audio sources. Making a 'top ten' music hits tape, with you as the DJ, may be easy but it will not challenge you very much. If you are making a radio programme you should think about a 5–10-minute section of a radio-style

TIP

You can hear some school radio projects by following the links on Heinemann Hotlinks. They are not all GCSE standard, but you can get an idea of the type of radio work going on in schools around the country. Listen to some of the productions and discuss with other members of your group how they could have been improved.

magazine programme. This will enable you to play some music but, most importantly, to include a variety of speech-based material.

For some sections of the programme you may actually script a whole piece, word for word. Reading out a script and making it sound spontaneous is actually very difficult, however, so for much of the time you might just use cue cards which help you with ideas and links between items but which are not word perfect. You can find more advice about making links on page 146.

When writing your programme outline, you should think about how you can introduce as much variety as possible. The speech items can be presented in a number of different ways.

● Use one main presenter to link the various sections of the programme together.

● Include interviews, possibly recorded on location, to give a different feel. The interviewer can ask questions of one or more guests.

● Some sections of the programme could be *two-headed* – two people present a piece together, as often seen on Breakfast TV shows.

You may play out some music tracks for their own sakes, but you should certainly think about using music as a 'bed' underneath some of the speech items.

With those points in mind, write up a running order and assemble all the music you will need.

Production

A great deal of radio output is live. The part of your programme which is most likely to be live will be the links between items you have pre-recorded, or between music tracks. Doing live links is a real skill which only comes with practice. Make sure you have practised this before you come to a live microphone and do the real thing.

At this stage of production, you will pre-record any interviews and other speech items. You can make your recordings on an audio cassette, a mini-disc recorder or even using just the audio recording facility of a digital video camera. The advantage of this is that many digital video-editing software packages have good sound-mixing and editing facilities that you could use in post-production.

Whatever type of recorder you use, there are two things you need to think about when recording: sound levels and location.

Sound levels

Ideally all the sound levels of your recordings should be similar so that your listeners are not straining to hear one item and deafened by the next. You can control this to some extent in post-production, but it is a good discipline to get the levels right at the recording stage. There are two ways to control sound level:

● *Distance from the microphone*: too far away and the sound will be faint, too close and you will hear all sorts of 'popping' where the force of breath on the microphone is picked up. Microphones perform differently so it is very important to experiment to find out the best position for yours.

● *Setting a recording level* (unless you are using a completely automatic machine): a light usually flashes on when sound is 'peaking'. The ideal recording level is when the 'peak' light only lights up very occasionally. If it stays on all the time, you are recording too much level, but if it never comes on at all, you are probably recording too little level.

Location

Sound engineers often talk about having a 'nice dry sound'. What they mean is the sound of a voice which feels close to the listener with little background noise or echo. To get 'dry' sound you need the microphone close to the mouth and a small room with lots of carpet and curtain to deaden down any echo. Of course, when you record interviews on location in the street, you will want background sounds – but not so loud that they drown out what is being said.

Post-production

This is the stage where you edit together the various audio sources you have collected during production. Follow your running order to ensure you put everything in the right place. Depending on the equipment you are using, you can also edit out any unwanted pauses or mistakes and mix speech items with music and sound effects.

You will need to use some form of *audio mixer* for this stage of your work. A mixer does literally what it says: it mixes together several different sound sources. You control the volume level of each by using *sound faders*. The faders allow you to have a music 'bed' running beneath the voice track. Depending on how much you pay and what you are using it for, a mixer can take anything from two to a hundred sources and mix them down to a single signal. If you have been recording using cassette tape then you will need an *analogue* mixing unit.

8 This student is using a good-quality sixteen-track mixer, but much simpler, cheaper mixing units will do perfectly well

For the purposes of your production work, three- or four-track mixing will be quite sufficient. Connect the microphone (or microphones if you are using more than one presenter) for your 'live' links to one input, a CD player for music tracks to another and the tape recorder or mini-disc player with your additional speech content to a third or fourth. You will then need another recording machine to connect to the output channel to capture the finished recording.

If you have recorded your sound on a digital recorder – either a mini-disc player or a video camera – then you can complete your post-production editing and mixing using digital software.

9 The three-channel sound-mixing facility on the Pinnacle Studio digital video-editing software can work perfectly well for mixing the sound for your radio project – as long as you have digital audio source material

The basic principles for digital mixing are the same as for the analogue process described above. You take three or four sources and balance the sound levels against each other to produce your final programme. The difference is that you will be doing all the mixing and editing on screen, so the actual operations you have to carry out will vary depending on the software package you are using. In most cases, however, you will see the sounds displayed as wave forms. You will move these along three or four timelines, raising and lowering the sound level by computer mouse clicks or drags. Cutting out unwanted sound is also very straightforward. Follow the instructions on the Help menus which come with the software, or use the instruction manual.

Printed media

This section is relevant if you are producing a newspaper or magazine or a multimedia advertising campaign which includes posters or display advertisements. There are two key things to consider when working in any of the print media forms:

● **The copy:** this is any sort of written material – the slogan on an advertisement or an article for a newspaper or magazine.

● **The layout:** this is the way pages are set out to attract reader's attention by visual impact. It includes use of photographs, graphics, typefaces and colour.

Pre-production

Your research should include a close examination of products similar to the one you are going to work on. Look at a range of magazines, newspapers or advertisements and make notes about these features.

● *Content:* What is the subject matter of the articles and the style in which they are written? Are they mainly presented as stories or are there a lot of interviews? How long is the average article? Do similar types of story appear in the same place in most publications?

- *Presentation:* How much of the publication is given over to photos? Are any drawings used? How many different styles of print are used? Are the colours bright and brash or muted and subtle?

- *Audience:* What kind of reader are the products aimed at? How do you know?

- *Front pages or covers:* These are a crucial part of any publication. They are the way potential readers are 'grabbed' as they look along the racks in newsagents. What does the front cover tell you about the sort of readership being targeted? What idea of the content of the magazine does the cover give? How does the combination of pictures and words encourage people to buy the publication? What kind of lifestyle is being catered for by this magazine?

- *Advertising:* newspapers and magazines need to sell advertising space to help cover the cost of production. What products are being advertised and what does this tell you about the sorts of readers being targeted?

Production

When you have decided on your target audience, draw up your production schedule. This is a list of all the things which need to be done, who will be doing them and the deadlines which need to be met.

Stage 1: Planning the content

Draw up a list of all the articles you wish to include and how many pages you can realistically produce in the time you have been given. It is much better to produce fewer high-quality pages than a lot of articles which are poorly written and badly laid out because you have tried to do too much in too short a space of time.

As a guideline, think in terms of each individual being responsible for two double-page spreads. The person responsible for the cover could count that as the equivalent of a double page. Anyone designing a full-page advertisement could also substitute that for a double-page spread.

Once you have a clear outline of what the finished product will look like, divide up the writing and photography tasks among the members of your group.

Stage 2: Writing the articles

You might be able to write some articles immediately, but others will need to be researched or require an interview to be arranged. You might decide at this stage that one of the group will act as a picture researcher. Their job will be to search the Internet and collect a range of pictures which might be useful for each article so that a wide choice is available at the page design stage.

Ideally you will have two *production meetings* where the whole group come together and review the work.

The first one should be halfway through the writing stage. The main purpose will be to check that everyone is running to time, and if not, take immediate action to make sure any problems are overcome. Are you able to extend your deadlines? If not, are you going to have to drop some articles? Will there be sufficient content left to ensure each group member can show how much they know about producing whatever product you have chosen to make? Are the pictures that have been collected appropriate?

The second production meeting will come at the end of the process of writing. You should all read each other's work in a productive, critical way and suggest any amendments which might be necessary. At this stage you should make a mock-up of the front page or cover and decide on a title for the paper or magazine. Anyone who has been designing a full-page advert should present their ideas at this meeting. Finally, you need to list any photographs that need to be taken.

Stage 3: Photo shoots

The photograph for the front cover of a magazine should be very carefully planned. Photographs used in advertisements also need to be thought through and a variety of alternatives taken from which the best one can be chosen.

For a professional fashion/advertisement shoot there will be a number of people involved:

- art director (in overall charge of the shoot)
- photographer (takes the photos and makes suggestions to the art director)
- two or three photographer's assistants to carry gear and set up lights
- stylist (to supervise costume and make-up)
- the client or their representative (to check they are happy with what is being photographed)
- the model or models.

You will probably have a much smaller crew, but you should certainly involve more than one person. Above all you need to look at every single detail of the images that you take to make sure that the photograph is conveying exactly the right message to your audience.

When posing any models for each photograph, use the following checklist:

- *Posture:* how will I pose the model? Lazing on a sofa will give a relaxed feel to the image; sitting upright in an office chair will give a more formal feel.
- *Facial expression:* do I want to create a moody look? Or do I want a happy, relaxed feel to the shot?
- *Costume:* what someone wears tells other people a great deal about them. Make sure that each piece of your model's clothing has been selected to get across the chosen image.
- *Setting and props:* think about the message that the setting of your shot will convey, and any props you use. Is the school playing field *really* the best setting for your jeans advert – or have you just gone there because it is easy? Is your teacher's N-reg. Fiesta going to add to the 'cool image' you are trying to create?

Once you have all of the things on that checklist sorted out, your next job is to compose them within the frame of your camera. Although there is no hard-and-fast set of rules about what makes a good photograph, the following composition guidelines might offer you a starting point for making interesting images.

Using thirds

Where will you place significant elements in your picture? Research has shown that viewers look first at the human face – especially the eyes – and any points of high contrast. Photographers often talk about the *principle of thirds*. When looking through the viewfinders of their cameras, they imagine a grid formed by two vertical and two horizontal lines which divide the picture into thirds. They then place key elements of the composition, often using a one-third to two-thirds proportion. Look at photograph **10** and think about the way it has used thirds for its composition.

10 This photo was composed using the principle of thirds

Lines of movement

Photographs are often thought to have a stronger composition if the objects in them are seen as 'moving into' the picture – see **11**.

11 The men are looking into the right of this frame

Diagonals and horizontals

Diagonal lines in compositions are said to be more dynamic than horizontal ones. How have lines been used in the composition in image **12**?

12 St Marks Square, Venice

Angle

Most photographs are taken at eye level. Taking them from above or below, as in **13**, your subject can be another way of creating visual impact.

13 This photo was taken from a low angle

Light

Getting the lighting right can mean more than just making sure there is enough light. The factors mentioned for video production on page 175 apply equally to lighting for a still photograph. Strong sunlight coming through the overhead railway in Brooklyn adds to the composition of photograph **14**.

14 Lighting is an important feature of this composition

Post-production

With your articles written and imagery produced, you now need to decide the order in which articles will appear and – crucially – how they are to be laid out on the page. It is the presentation of your publication that would sell it in the real world.

Using a computer software package at the page design stage will obviously be a great advantage as you can quickly and easily manipulate both your written work and your images. Being able to see the effect of changes in layout and font makes experimentation easy. However, you can still use older methods of cutting up and pasting your work directly onto paper. Remember: you should be thinking about the *appropriateness* of your design to your intended audience as well as how to grab and keep a reader's attention.

Some hints on layout

● Look at a wide range of different publications and make notes of layout features which you think would be good to incorporate in your production.

● Use a page grid to help you in your page design, even if you decide to break out of it. This is how all page designs in professional publications start out – see the example in **15**.

● The various parts of the design do not have to be straight or orderly. Scattered letters can add to the dynamic look of the page. However, if you use straight lines and columns, make sure they are just that!

● Use blank space. It can provide contrast in your design. If everything is spaced out evenly it can look bland and uninteresting.

● Titles set on a diagonal can add emphasis and look more dynamic.

● If your production is using a double-page spread which is to be folded and stapled, make a small dummy version that includes the same number of pages. Number the pages, then separate them to see which page goes with which on the paste-up. You can see the page combinations for a sixteen-page booklet in image **16**.

				Here we would have the text of our article.	A photo could go here.	
				THIS MIGHT BE A MAJOR TITLE		
				Here we would have the text of our article.	Here we would have the text of our article.	Here we would have the text of our article.
						A photo could go here.

15 A layout grid gives a starting point onto which the design can be plotted

| 13 | 4 1 | 16 | **side 1** |
| 12 | 5 8 | 9 | |

| 11 | 6 7 | 10 | **side 2** |
| 14 | 3 2 | 15 | |

16 Page combinations for a sixteen-page publication

17 A student's practical production

PERCY PIG AND FRIENDS

For my GCSE production piece, I decided to create a new unisex comic aimed at 4–6-year-olds called 'Percy Pig and Friends'.

Before I made my comic, I researched other comics aimed at a similar age range of children, such as 'Fireman Sam', 'The Tweenies' and 'Teletubbies'. I noticed that they all used similar conventions such as bright colours, simple, easy-to-recognise characters (which often had intertextual links to television programmes) and activities to encourage children to read, write and solve problems.

I wanted my ideas to be completely original, and so did not base my comic characters on any other media texts, but I could imagine that if my comic was successful, it would be a simple step to create a cartoon series around the characters.

In order to make my front cover appealing, I drew Percy Pig as the central image. He looks happy and friendly, and is using direct mode of address to look straight at the audience as if to say, 'You're my friend too' (this links with the title 'Percy Pig and Friends'). The simple background of hills and sheep with Percy standing in a puddle of mud suggests a farmyard, country setting which young children often find fascinating. The other characters, Cammy the Cow, Blot the Dog, Wilma the Sheep and Hetty Hen, reinforce this, offering lots of opportunities for stories to develop around each of them in future.

I understand that it is not only children who are the target audience for a comic like mine, since it must also appeal to the adults who would be paying for the comic. For this reason I have ensured that there are plenty of clues to the educational content of the comic on the front page, with puffs at the bottom suggesting that there are stories, puzzles and colouring activities inside. These include 'spot the difference', a matching game, hide and seek and colour-in-Cammy. There is also a letters page inside featuring children's pictures and letters and a competition to win Magic Colour modelling clay. These are all typical features of a comic like this.

I have also created a bookmark as a free gift incentive to the buyer – a useful, educational item which children will be able to use when they are reading stories (either by themselves or with adults), and which will also remind them of their favourite comic since Percy and his friends are all featured on it. This would be a good way to ensure they will want the next edition of the comic.

Other features to encourage new readers are, firstly, that it is the first ever issue (indicated by the buzz word 'New!' and 'No. 1' next to the price), so adults and children will feel they are having something exclusive and new, and will be able to collect future editions without missing any adventures. Secondly, the price of 95p is very competitive compared to other comics aimed at a similar audience, and I do feel it is offering value for money.

I have tried to make my front cover look as 'real' as possible, by following comic conventions and layout conventions that other comics and magazines use, such as a bar code, and a message referring to the free gift and what to do if it is not attached to the front page.

I drew the front cover myself, because I wanted to achieve a friendly 'graphic style' for the characters, and I am very pleased with the overall effect. Having used pencil and inks, I was a little disappointed by the fading of some colours after I had the pages colour photocopied, and had to go over some of the lines in black. If I had access to more sophisticated printing technology with a graphics pad, for example, this could be avoided.

Overall, I am very pleased with my comic. I feel it does look convincing and would appeal to its target audience of 4–6-year-old boys and girls.

18 The evaluation for the practical production in **17**

Completing your practical media production work

The final stage of the practical media production work is the completion of the written evaluation of your finished piece of work. You should have been building up a commentary as your project progressed, highlighting the major decisions which were made at each stage. Now it is time to step back and look with fresh eyes at what you have produced. You can see an example in **18**.

Examiner's tips

- Use some of the guidance given in this unit to help you comment on decisions you made, for example: *We used just one strong light set to the side of the actor in this shot to create a sinister mood.*

- Make connections between your work and the key concepts of the GCSE Media Studies specification, for example: *We photographed the image of Ella carefully, dressing her in that powerful way to represent a strong, assertive female, breaking the stereotype of women as always dependent on men for everything.*

- Above all – *evaluate* your production. The difference between students getting high marks and the rest is the quality of their evaluation. Does your supporting account make judgements about how effectively your work met its intended purpose? The rest of your course will have taught you how to evaluate professional media products. Use these skills on your own practical media production work.

UNIT SUMMARY

Key area	What you have learned
Media language	• The importance of using your chosen media technologies to produce a high-quality finish appropriate to the task you set yourself.
Audiences	• That all media products must be targeted carefully at a target audience if they are to be successful.
Institutions and organisations	• That although you may not be able to match the level of finish achieved by the professionals, they will have followed the same processes as you have in your work.
Representation	• That whatever you have chosen to film, photograph or record, you will have represented the ideas, issues and people in a particular way. Another group could have presented a completely different representation of the same subject matter.

Before you start, make sure you read and understand the information about the coursework assignments given on pages 9–12.

The suggestions for coursework assignments in this section are offered as an example only – there are many other avenues you could explore. The important thing is to ensure that your coursework folder contains the right balance of pieces, that you stick to the word counts and that they meet the necessary assessment criteria. You are required to produce three coursework assignments, plus a practical production and supporting account. You will find details of all these areas in the AQA introduction. Look in Unit 9 Succeeding with Practical Media Production Work for useful support for the practical aspects of your assignment.

Area of study: Film promotion and distribution

This assignment will focus on moving image and print-based texts.

In this assignment you will:
- Explore the ways films are promoted
- Compare two posters for films of different genres
- Design publicity material for a new film

Section One: Explore the ways films are promoted

This part of your assignment will help you to meet the assessment objectives on Knowledge and Understanding (AO1). It will address Key Concepts:

- Audience

- Institutions

Imagine you are part of a film distribution team devising a promotion package for a new blockbuster called *Finders Keepers* (a fictional film for which you invent the details).

Write about 300 words describing your ideas for promoting the film. Where appropriate, explain why your strategy for marketing the film will gain the maximum response from the public. Look back at Unit 1 Film pages 25–32 to remind yourself of the various ways that films are promoted. Set out your ideas under these headings:

- **Background:** This gives a brief description of the genre and plot, e.g.:
  Romantic comedy: Two city dwellers meet at a lost property office and soon quarrel over who has lost a leather briefcase … but will they find love?

  Horror: When Sarah moves into her new house she finds more than cobwebs in the attic – has she found them or have they found her?

- **Cast:** Now think about the stars you want to be in the film and explain why your chosen actors will attract a particular audience to the film.

- **Release date:** Is this movie to be a summer event or linked to a particular public holiday such as Christmas?

- **Teaser materials:** Two or three months ahead of the release, you may want to circulate posters and trailers to generate interest. What would you include in them? How would they work to interest your audience?
- **Cinema release:** Will the film open in all cinemas at the same time or will you target the bigger cities first?
- **Celebrity appearances:** Think about how you could use the stars of your film – for example: for television appearances, the premiere, film festivals and themed parties – to attract the attention of the press and public.

Section Two: Compare two posters for films of different genres

This part of your assignment will help you meet the assessment objectives on Analysis and Interpretation (AO2). It will address Key Concepts:

- Media Language
- Audience
- Representation

Choose two film posters from contrasting genres and explain how they:

a)   **convey meaning to the audience**

b)   **attract interest in the film.**

Look back at Unit 1 Film pages 25–26 for ideas about analysing film posters. You could use the posters in **1** and **2** on pages 196 and 197 or any suitable posters from Unit 1 in your comparison. In your assignment you may consider:

- The gesture codes of the actor(s)
- Clothes, location/setting (mise-en-scene)
- The use of objects/colour
- The tag line
- Written information about the director/cast/studio
- How the audience is positioned – how is the viewer being invited to react?
- Are men and women represented in any particular way, e.g. as tough guys or damsels in distress?
- Are all the actors from the same racial group?

Section Three: Design publicity material for a new film

This part of your assignment will help you meet the assessment objectives on Production Skills (AO3). It will address Key Concepts:

- Audience
- Representation
- Media Language

Design either a poster or a trailer for your film *Finders Keepers*. Remember to apply the relevant codes and conventions.

- Look at a variety of film posters in film magazines, such as *Empire*, or visit your local video store to see the posters on display.
- Decide where the images will be positioned and what background colour will be appropriate to the genre. Choose an appropriate font size and style. Include a tag line which invites your audience to choose to see the film. This could be in the form of a question or unfinished statement followed by ellipsis (…).
- Produce your poster using a computer if possible. You should produce at least three different designs; in your evaluation you could discuss the strengths and weaknesses of each design. Label your designs to show their features. The evaluation for the poster might include a brief description of what you have made and who the target audience is.
- If you choose to design a trailer, remind yourself of the conventions by viewing a variety of trailers. You can find these on shop-bought videos and DVDs. Remember that many trailers have a voice-over which gives information and encourages the audience to see the film. Look back at Unit 1 Film pages 29–30 for more support.
- You may present your trailer in storyboard form or as a fully realised production. You could use your knowledge of media language here as you could take the opportunity to describe camera shots and show how sound and dialogue fit into the whole set-up (see Unit 9 Succeeeding with Practical Media Production Work). Remember to draw your storyboard in pencil, using black pen for camera angles and shot length.

The evaluation might include:

- A brief description of what you have made and who the target audience is
- An explanation of the genre and narrative of the piece
- A section to show your knowledge of video production using editing terminology and pointing out how you achieved the soundtrack
- Some comments that point out the strengths and weaknesses of your work.

1 *Pleasantville* (1998) (See Section Two on page 194)

10 Coursework assignments: Film

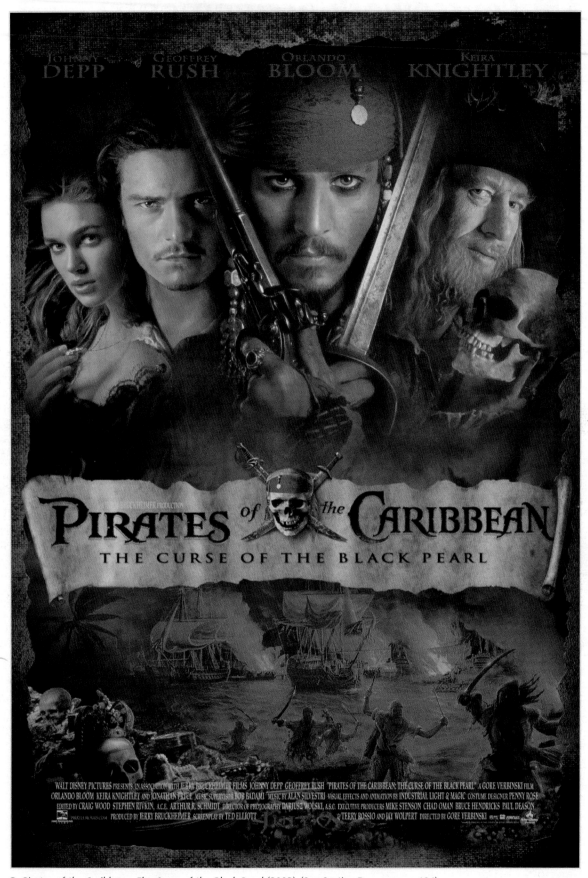

2 *Pirates of the Caribbean: The Curse of the Black Pearl* (2003) (See Section Two on page 194)

11 Coursework assignments: Television

Before you start, make sure you read and understand the information about the coursework assignments given on pages 9–12.

The suggestions for coursework assignments in this section are offered as an example only – there are many other avenues you could explore. The important thing is to ensure that your coursework folder contains the right balance of pieces, that you stick to the word counts and that they meet the necessary assessment criteria. You are required to produce three coursework assignments, plus a practical production and supporting account. You will find details of all these areas in the AQA introduction. Look in Unit 9 Succeeding with Practical Media Production Work for useful support for the practical aspects of your assignment.

Area of study: Situation comedy

This assignment will focus on moving image texts.

In this assignment you will:
- Explore the conventions of situation comedy
- Analyse the presentation of family life in a chosen sitcom
- Create ideas for a new sitcom

Section One: Explore the conventions of situation comedy
This part of your assignment will help you to meet the assessment objectives on Knowledge and Understanding (AO1). It will address Key Concepts:

- Media Language – narrative and genre

- Audience

Using examples you have viewed and researched, describe the main features of the sitcom genre.

Look back at the material on situation comedy in Unit 2 Television pages 50–54 before you start this assignment. Then watch several sitcoms and decide what are the forms and conventions of the genre. In your description you could include references to:

- How the narratives are structured – does something happen that creates a chain of events?
- Their settings and characters – is humour derived from the type of person and where they are, e.g. a difficult boss in the workplace?
- How physical and verbal humour is used.
- The pleasures of the text for the audience – do they feel superior to the characters or do they identify with them? This would be an opportunity to apply the Uses and Gratifications theory (see page 88).

Section Two: Analyse the presentation of family life in a chosen sitcom

This part of your assignment will help you to meet assessment objectives on Analysis and Interpretation (AO2). It will address the Key Concept:

● Representation

> **View one episode of a family-based sitcom and comment on the representation of parents and children. Can you identify any stereotypes presented in it?**
>
> Think about the mother and father in the episode. Which is presented as being the most powerful? Does the programme show the family unit as harmonious and if not, what are the sources of the problems?

Section Three: Create ideas for a new sitcom

This part of your assignment will help you meet assessment objectives on Production Skills (AO3). It will address Key Concepts:

● Media language – narrative and genre
● Representation

> **Write a treatment for a new sitcom based on school or sixth-form college life.**
>
> A treatment is a proposal that outlines the features of a possible new programme. In your treatment you could:
>
> • Give the opening episode character profiles of up to six main pupil characters.
> • Describe three contrasting teachers to feature in the pilot episode.
> • Outline three possible storylines.
> • Design the opening credits.
>
> Before you write your treatment, do some careful preparation work. Watch a selection of sitcoms and soaps about teenagers. Research your audience – you could carry out a survey of students in your school to find out which sitcoms they find amusing. Then:
>
> • decide on the age of your audience
> • decide at what time and on what channel your sitcom will be shown.
>
> Your treatment may have more chance of being accepted if you can suggest which advertisers might find your programme attractive.
>
> Try to reflect a multi-cultural society and think of ways you can avoid relying on traditional sitcom stereotypes like the 'battleaxe' (the bossy older woman).

Coursework assignments: Newspapers

Before you start, make sure you read and understand the information about the coursework assignments given on pages 9–12.

The suggestions for coursework assignments in this section are offered as an example only – there are many other avenues you could explore. The important thing is to ensure that your coursework folder contains the right balance of pieces, that you stick to the word counts and that they meet the necessary assessment criteria. You are required to produce three coursework assignments, plus a practical production and supporting account. You will find details of all these areas in the AQA introduction. Look in Unit 9 Succeeding with Practical Media Production Work for useful support for the practical aspects of your assignment.

Area of study: Newspaper front pages

This assignment will focus on print-based text.

In this assignment you will:
- Compare the different ways two newspapers cover the same story on their front pages, making clear why you think the differences have occurred
- Compare the ways the two newspapers write about the story on their inside pages
- Produce the lead stories for the front pages of two tabloids that take different viewpoints on the same story, including a photograph and a headline for each

Section One: Comparing how the front pages of two newspapers cover the same story

This part of your assignment will help you to meet the assessment objectives on Knowledge and Understanding (AO1) and Analysis and Interpretation (AO2). It will address Key Concepts:

- Representation

- Media Language

- Institutions

Compare the way that front pages of the *Daily Mirror* and the *Daily Express* covered the story of Princess Diana's butler, Paul Burrell, in November 2002.

Look first at the two front pages in **1** and **2**. Look back at the material on newspaper front pages on pages 68–74 of Unit 3 Newspapers. Before you write up your comparison, make notes about the following points:

- **Headlines:** How well do the headlines work in grabbing the reader's attention? What *angle* or *point of view* is each paper putting forward about the butler?
- **Photographs:** How have photographs been used on the front page of each paper? What do you think was the source of the *Daily Mirror's* photograph? Why do you think the *Daily Express* did not use a photograph of Burrell?

- **Layout:** Comment on the overall design of the page, including the balance of words to pictures, and how effective you think it will be in holding the reader's attention.
- **News values:** Why do you think this story was included as the front-page lead in both these newspaper? You could consider using the work of Galtung and Ruge (see page 79).

1 *Daily Mirror*, 5 November 2002

DAILY EXPRESS

CRUSADING FOR A SAFER BRITAIN   The World's Greatest Newspaper   TUESDAY NOVEMBER 5, 2002   20p

ONLY 20p TODAY

JAMIE OLIVER EXCLUSIVE
PAGES 24&25
PLUS: Food to help you stay young
THE ORACLE DIET SEE PAGE 29

95p OFF OK!
BRITAIN'S NUMBER 1 CELEBRITY MAGAZINE

Including free HOT STARS PAGE 52

FREE INSIDE: FANTASTIC PULL-OUT CHRISTMAS TRAVEL SPECIAL

BUTLER BETRAYS DIANA'S MEMORY

We reveal sordid secrets Burrell sold for cash

BUTLER Paul Burrell is to sell the sordid secrets of his life with Princess Diana for up to £1million.

He plans to betray her memory by accepting lucrative offers from TV and a downmarket tabloid newspaper.

The revelations of Diana's most trusted servant are said to be an "hon-

By Cyril Dixon

est and searing account" which contains damning criticism of senior royals, including Prince Philip.

Burrell, 44, has consistently refused to reveal details of his life below stairs and has criticised former aides who

told all. But his sensational secrets have leaked out and are published in the Daily Express today.

Burrell cashed in quickly because he feared that further leaks would seriously reduce the value of his story.

Last night's confirmation of two big

TURN TO PAGE 4, COLUMN 3

EXCLUSIVE
Mary Archer: Jeffrey and his affairs
PAGE 11

EXCLUSIVE

Posh in hiding after family kidnap scare
PAGES 8&9

OPINION **12** LETTERS **26** DIARY **27** EXPRESS WOMAN **29-43** TV **47-50** OBITS **52** CROSSWORD **53** STARS **55** CITY **56-60** SPORT **61-72**

2 *Daily Express,* 5 November 2002

Section Two: Comparing the stories on the inside pages

This part of your assignment will help you to meet the assessment objectives on Knowledge and Understanding (AO1) and Analysis and Interpretation (AO2). It will address Key Concepts:

● Representation

● Institutions

Compare the ways the two newspapers write about the Burrell story on their inside pages.

Now look at the articles from the inside pages of the two papers in **3** and **4**. To help you make this comparison you should comment on:

• **Fact and opinion**: What *facts* do you find that are common to both articles? Are there any things that ought to be facts which are different in the articles? Explore the amount of *opinion* compared to fact which each article contains.

• **Angle** and **use of emotive language**: Examine the particular *angle* that is followed through in the articles. You should comment particularly on the material each paper has selected to support the angle it has taken. How has each paper used emotive language to support the way they represent the story?

• Finally, you need to think about the question of **Media Institutions**. Why do you think one seems to be more sympathetic to Paul Burrell than the other?

BUTLER SPEAKS OUT ONLY IN THE MIRROR

It is the one story the world wants to hear – Paul Burrell's searing account of one of the most amazing episodes involving the Royal Family.

Starting tomorrow only in the *Daily Mirror*, Princess Diana's butler will tell what really happened at THAT meeting with the Queen which cleared his name.

He will reveal his true feelings about the princess's Spencer family and how they "wanted to crush the Rock".

He will tell of his near two-year anguish when falsely accused of stealing royal items and his joy when the monarch confirmed his innocence.

The man who stood by Diana in life and pledged never to betray her in death will also disclose the real story of the Diana Memorial Fund and the battles he faced.

Speaking for the first time since he walked free from the Old Bailey four days ago Paul, 44, said: "This is my story – my turn to put the record straight, settle a few scores and correct many lies.

"It will be the truth, the whole truth and nothing but the truth, something I never got to say in court."

It is a mark of the man that Paul's story has not gone to the highest bidder, despite the financial ruin the theft case brought him.

Snubbing offers of more than £1million he has chosen the *Mirror* in which to open his heart because, he said, it is the "people's paper". He said: "I've chosen a path which is the best one to tell a story with dignity and honesty. This was never about money. I'm not interested in making the most amount that I can.

3 *Daily Mirror*, 5 November 2002

Butler betrays Diana's memory

We reveal sordid secrets
Burrell sold for cash

Butler Paul Burrell is to sell the sordid secrets of his life with Princess Diana for up to £1million.

He plans to betray her memory by accepting lucrative offers from TV and a downmarket tabloid newspaper.

The revelations of Diana's most trusted servant are said to be an "honest and searing account" which contains damning criticism of senior royals, including Prince Philip.

Burrell, 44, consistently refused to reveal details of his life below stairs and has criticised former aides who told all. But his sensational secrets have leaked out and are published in the *Daily Express* today.

Burrell cashed in quickly because he feared that further leaks would seriously reduce the value of his story.

Last night's confirmation of two big deals came 24 hours after his brother Graham said he was out for revenge.

Details of Burrell's ordeal leading up to the Old Bailey case will emerge in a TV video diary recorded by Granada's *Tonight* with Trevor McDonald. Further deals with foreign publications are also being negotiated.

The father-of-two, who Diana described as her "Rock", was shadowed by cameramen during the final six months before his acquittal of theft charges on Friday.

4 *Daily Express*, 5 November 2002

Section Three: Produce the lead stories for the front pages of two tabloids with different viewpoints

This part of your assignment will help you to meet the assessment objective on Production Skills (AO3). It will address Key Concepts:

● Media Language

● Institutions

● Audience

Produce the lead stories for the front pages of two tabloids that take different viewpoints on the same story. For each front page you should include a masthead, a headline, at least one photograph, and up to 80 words of copy.

In designing your front pages you should refer back to the material on layout in Unit 3 Newspapers (pages 68–74) and try to incorporate as many features as possible.

• Re-read carefully the section on print media on pages 183–188 in Unit 9 Succeeding with Practical Media Production Work.

• First decide on the content of your story. Try to think of a story for which you can produce your own photographs.

• Try to think of a good reason *why* the papers hold opposing views – this will be useful in your evaluation.

• In your pre-production work you can produce several page layouts, labelled with the features, and a choice of photographs. Explain your choices in your evaluation.

Coursework assignments: Magazines and comics

Before you start, make sure you read and understand the information about the coursework assignments given on pages 9–12.

The suggestions for coursework assignments in this section are offered as an example only – there are many other avenues you could explore. The important thing is to ensure that your coursework folder contains the right balance of pieces, that you stick to the word counts and that they meet the necessary assessment criteria. You are required to produce three coursework assignments, plus a practical production and supporting account. You will find details of all these areas in the AQA introduction. Look in Unit 9 Succeeding with Practical Media Production Work for useful support for the practical aspects of your assignment.

Area of study: Magazine advertisements

This assignment will focus on print-based text.

In this assignment you will:
- Explore the links between the articles and the advertisements in a magazine
- Compare two advertisements from the same magazine
- Design and produce your own advertisement

Section One: Explore the links between the articles and the advertisements in a magazine

This part of your assignment will help you to meet the assessment objectives on Knowledge and Understanding (AO1). It will address Key Concepts:

● Audience

● Institutions

Using a magazine of your choice, explore the links between the articles or stories and the advertisements that appear within it.

First look back at pages 163–165 in Unit 8 Advertising for information on advertising in magazines. Then choose a magazine with a good range of articles and advertisements to make your analysis more interesting.

When you do this task you need to think about why an advertiser would choose to buy advertising space in this particular comic or magazine. This will clearly have something to do with the audience for the publication you have chosen, and this in turn depends on the content of the articles or stories in it. People do not buy magazines for the advertisements – they buy them to enjoy the articles.

First, make a list of all the contents of the publication, excluding the advertisements. When you have completed that survey, see if you can find advertisements that are linked in some way to the themes or topics of the articles. Set out your findings in a chart like the one at the top of the next page.

MAGAZINE: _____

Title of article	Brief description of content	Advert that links to this
Zit, zit, zit	*How to deal with acne*	*Nospotz acne cream*

Write about 300 words that report on what you have found out. When doing this you should:

● Comment on why you think the articles will appeal to the target readership of the magazine.

● Describe any advertisements you found that had a link with the articles, explaining what the link was.

● Explain why you think that advertisers and magazine editors would agree to make these sorts of links.

Section Two: Compare two advertisements from the same magazine

This part of your assignment will help you to meet the assessment objectives on Analysis and Interpretation (AO2). It will address Key Concepts:

● Audience

● Representation

● Media Language

Compare the way these two advertisements from the same magazine for teenage girls target apparently different audiences and explore why this might be the case.

Both advertisements **1** and **2** come from the same edition of an American magazine for teenage girls.

In setting up the photographs that have been used in these advertisements, the Art Director will have planned every last detail of each shot. They are trying to make sure that people who see the advertisement react in the way that the client company would want them to – what is called *positioning* the audience.

Your comparison should include comments about the following list of points, all of which will have been carefully controlled during the photo shoot:

• the character types portrayed by the models
• their facial expressions
• their gestures or posture
• the types of clothes they are wearing
• any props in the photograph
• the location or setting that has been used.
• What is the effect of the type of shot (long shot, medium shot, close up, etc.)?
• Why was the shot composed in this way? What effect do any aspects of the colour used in the design have?

1 Advertisement for Gasoline jeans from an American teenage magazine

2 This clothing advertisement appeared in the same issue as **1**

You could then consider *how* and *why* these techniques target the audiences for the advertisements.

- When all the above points have been combined, what ideas or emotions do you think the creative team hoped to conjure up in their audience by the way they have constructed each image?
- What *representation* is the reader offered of male and female gender in each image?
- In trying to sell us the particular line of clothing, what ideas and values are also being 'sold' to the reader as desirable?
- Lastly, having thought about all those things, who do you think the target *audience* is for each advertisement? How do you know this?

Section Three: Design and produce your own magazine advertisement

This part of your assignment will help you to meet the assessment objectives on Production Skills (AO3). It will address Key Concepts:

- Audience

- Representation

- Media Language

Design an advertisement for a product of your choice, stating clearly the type of publication you would place it in and the target audience it addresses.

When planning your advertisement, you should consider all the things which you looked at on the list given in Section Two.

Research the advertisements in similar magazines. Draft at least three possible designs. You could create the designs using a computer or by hand. Label the designs with notes to draw attention to such things as persuasive techniques and key features. This will allow you to show your understanding of these areas without using up your evaluation word limit. Remember to consider:

- the target audience
- the mode of address
- where the advert will be placed.

In your evaluation explain why you chose the final design, how this design targets the audience and is suitable for the type of publication. You could suggest any improvements you could make if you had more resources.

Before you start, make sure you read and understand the information about the coursework assignments given on pages 9–12.

The suggestions for coursework assignments in this section are offered as an example only – there are many other avenues you could explore. The important thing is to ensure that your coursework folder contains the right balance of pieces, that you stick to the word counts and that they meet the necessary assessment criteria. You are required to produce three coursework assignments, plus a practical production and supporting account. You will find details of all these areas in the AQA introduction. Look in Unit 9 Succeeding with Practical Media Production Work for useful support for the practical aspects of your assignment.

Area of study – the pop video

This assignment will focus on moving image texts.

In this assignment you will:
- Explore the importance of the pop video as a marketing tool
- Analyse the appeal of a specific pop video
- Create your own pop video

Section One: Explore the importance of the pop video as a marketing tool

This part of your assignment will help you to meet the assessment objectives on Knowledge and Understanding (AO1). It will address Key Concepts:

● Institutions

● Audience

Explain the importance of the pop video in promoting and marketing the work of a pop star or band. Use at least three examples you have seen and refer to the development of the genre over time.

In preparation for this assignment, view a variety of pop videos, both recent examples and texts from the past. As you watch, think about:

- A pop video's purpose as an advertisement
- Where it can be heard or seen
- Its appeal to audiences
- Its appeal to television producers, e.g. when artists may not be available in person
- Significant events in its development, e.g. the launch of MTV in 1981.